Experience Matters

"I've worked with Buddy since the very early days of Solutions 21. Among the reasons we have maintained a close connection over the years is Buddy's intense interest in helping others succeed. He has an inherent ability to accurately read the environment and honestly access a situation, which has enabled him to consistently deliver timely and valuable advice and services."
> – Steve Kontra, Regional Learning Leader Americas
> Pfizer Inc.

"We have worked with Buddy and Solutions 21 for nearly a decade. They have helped us with our long-term plan and developing our key people. I would venture to say we would not be where we are today without their help. They are a vital part of our business; lessons we have learned from Buddy and his team have become a critical part of our everyday processes."
> – Doug Dickler
> Sr. Director, Sales Operations & Business Intelligence
> Johnson & Johnson Consumer

"Over the years we have worked with many consultants. For a major project a few years ago we interviewed several people, including Buddy and his team. They were the perfect choice for our business. Buddy knows how to produce results AND how to connect with people. Our team found the process very helpful and profitable. In fact, following our initial planning sessions my team decided that Buddy actually undersold himself in the initial interviews. He was clearly the best choice for our business and our team. It is exciting to know he will be sharing those secrets with others. If you are thinking about a career as a consultant, then this is where you need to start your journey."
> – Jack Ouellette, President and CEO
> American Textile

"Having taught a seminar on how to be a successful consultant for over 25 years, I was surprised at how well this book dealt with the questions that new consultants have been asking. Advanced consultants will learn a thing or two as well, especially about selling their services."
> – Rick Crandall, author
> *Marketing for Consultants Who Hate to Sell*

"Our team has worked with Buddy and his team on various occasions. They have always been able to offer tools and insights that have helped us communicate more effectively and have helped our teams continue to grow and develop. In fact, many of the tools have helped so much we have been using them in several other areas of our business."
— David Jaffe, President and CEO
Ascena Retail Group, Inc.

"We truly consider Buddy and his team to be our business partner. For over 15 years we have worked with them on everything from business development to strategic planning and they have always produced quantifiable results. If Buddy is teaching folks how to be a consultant, then the consulting world is about to have a first-class teacher. If I were starting a consulting practice, this book would be the first investment for my practice."
— Thomas B. Grealish, President
Henderson Brothers, Inc.

"We have worked successfully with Buddy Hobart and his team over the years. Buddy possesses the unique talent of identifying the core issue of any situation every time. His latest literary effort is another example of his identifying a significant need and supplying a common-sense remedy. "
— Dan Salak, Senior Vice President
ASK Chemicals LP

"Experience does matter and this book is right on target. Having spent many years as a consultant myself I wish these insights were available to me when I was getting started. Buddy brings real-world practical advice to our company, and he is offering the 'solopreneur' that same opportunity with this book."
— Stephen D'Angelo, President
dck worldwide

"Buddy and his team have worked with our leaders from around the world. We like it when they bring us the tools. The processes they introduced to us work. In fact, I use many of the leadership tools personally and am surprised at how much I enjoy it. I clearly see how it helps us to align our global management practices."
— Jesper Jensen, CEO
JENSEN Group

Experience Matters

How to Succeed as a Consultant in Today's World

BUDDY HOBART

Select Press

Published by Select Press,
Novato, CA

ISBN 978-1-890777-54-8 Hard cover
ISBN 978-1-890777-55-5 Soft cover

Printed in USA

Dedication

To my wife Sue. Experience Matters in life and in business. As we have often discussed, it is how we finish the race that counts. I am blessed and grateful that you chose to run life's race with me as your partner.

CONTENTS

Preface

This book is intended to help consultants, especially those we work with through Ex3 Matters.

I hope both new and experienced consultants find it helpful, perhaps in different ways, whether you are an Ex3 Matters member or not.

Consulting is a very doable career for the right people, but it requires serious work. I hope this information helps you create the future you deserve.

Looking forward to meeting you in the field.

Buddy Hobart
(bhobart@ex3matters.com)

CHAPTER 1

A Major Opportunity for Consultants

The purpose of this book is to briefly discuss how to be successful in the field of consulting. Because of an unusual set of circumstances, the next few years are a key time to start a consulting career. And I happen to be in a position to recognize the new opportunity as well as offer general advice about being a consultant.

Why should you listen to me? I don't claim to be the best consultant in the world, and I don't represent the biggest firms you may have heard of like Bain, McKinsey, or Accenture. But I and my firm (Solutions 21) have provided consulting services since 1994. We achieved $1 million in revenues after three years in business and have been a multimillion-dollar firm ever since.

With offices in Pittsburgh and Phoenix, at any one time we may have 25–30 consultants on engagements, and we have served 50+ clients every year for many years. We have worked on assignments that have rescued dying companies, expanded firms 1700%, opened shuttered manufacturing plants, quadrupled the number of employees, implemented programs that made employees feel more valued, created strategic plans that produced some "best ever" performances – and that is just a sample. We have served clients like Heinz, Bayer, Schering-Plough, Dress Barn, Merck, USX, and Pfizer. We have worked on four continents and with people from 35 countries. Many of our clients have been with us almost from the beginning and have used us on projects *every* year, and we get much of our business from referrals. Sometimes our problem is not finding business but finding competent consultants to do the work.

Personally, I've written a couple of books that ended up giving me some insight into the current situation that consultants can take advantage of. And I've done proprietary research on world-class performers in many areas that's given me information about the traits and habits of very successful people. (This is covered in Chapter 2.)

I believe the time is right for experienced professionals to join the ranks of independent consultants. If you have years of experience as a professional and you are unemployed, underemployed, or want to try something new, NOW is the time to make your move. I will show you how you can take your experience and become a "solopreneur" consultant; the market is demanding your skills.

In 2009 I finished writing a book called *Gen Y Now: How Generation Y Changes Your Workplace* and *Why It Requires a New Leadership Style*. The research for that book and the subsequent consulting we have done have given me some new insights into the current work world. We have discovered there is a dramatic shift occurring in regards to how businesses

SOLOPRENEUR: Someone who is an independent professional, free agent, self-employed; chooses to go into business for him/herself; connects and builds alliances with others for collaboration according to needs.

obtain talent. This shift is not temporary. It is here to stay. It is the "new normal" and it is a huge opportunity for independent consultants.

The Baby Boomers – those born between 1946 and 1964 – have been the dominant generation in this country since the 1960s. As discussed in my last book (*GenY Now*), Boomers' dominance is waning as they age and leave the workforce. On January 1, 2011 the first of the Baby Boomers turned 65. This makes 1/1/11 a demographic "tipping point." For the next 18 years, 10,000 Americans a day will turn 65, one every 8½ seconds.

Knowledge Capital Needed!

In addition to ever increasing Baby Boomer retirements, millions of Boomers were downsized in the recession and are now unemployed. Most firms will not re-employ them and many Boomers have simply given up on becoming fully re-employed at their prerecession incomes doing the type of work they used to do.

As discussed in the February 19, 2012, "60 Minutes" show, there is now discrimination against the unemployed! Many job postings clearly state that only "currently employed" individuals will be considered.

There are four parts to why a strong need for consultants exist at this time. The first two parts, retirement and unemployment, are only the beginning. The third part is that many Baby Boomers and Gen X'ers, after months of searching for a new job at the previous levels of income and job responsibilities, chose to accept underemployment. (Underemployed means not doing work that makes full use of skills and abilities and not being paid an income equal to or more than previously earned.) Many very talented folks are making far less money than they did prior to the recession. This group MAY OR MAY NOT have less responsibility. In either case, this group tends to feel very unfulfilled at work.

This leads us to the fourth part of the equation, the unengaged workforce. To put it bluntly, many talented professionals hate their jobs. We have found three main reasons for these feelings:

1) When the recession began, some who did not lose their jobs did accept pay freezes and loss of substantial benefits. In addition to frozen incomes, at work they were forced to do "more with less" because they did lose

coworkers. Over time they have become overwhelmed and stressed due to the economic pressures and the sense of being "put upon." They feel a bit used, if not burnt out.

2) After losing their jobs, some found other positions doing similar work for much less pay. These folks tended to believe "if I can only prove myself, then they will see my value and pay me more fairly." What tended to happen is that they did prove themselves (and many times as a thank you, they received more work!) but did not receive significantly increased wages. One person I spoke to told me "all it did was confirm how big a bargain I am and now I am killing myself in the process."

3) After losing their jobs, others found work that really did not excite them or leverage their years of experience and know-how. This group is just plain bored.

A new kind of "brain drain" is occurring. Businesses are going to experience an exodus of talent. As many as two million workers a month are leaving their positions voluntarily. These folks are finding new work where the grass appears greener.

This exodus will only help independent consultants who can bridge the gap of lost knowledge capital. Businesses will increasingly demand "just-in-time" experience to fill this void. With employers leaving due to retirement, burnout, and other career opportunities, the market for independent talent will boom.

Why Become an Independent Consultant NOW?

The time is right to become a consultant now because timing is everything.

Despite the negative events that have happened to these experienced unemployed and underemployed Boomers, this group now has big, new opportunities in consulting.

Right after starting Solutions 21, I wrote a book called *Hire Education.* It was designed to help college students market themselves to prospective employers. For a few years prior to writing the book, I had lectured at colleges and universities around the country on the subject and enjoyed working with the students. The audience seemed to appreciate the information, and it was a needed subject. In 1999 the book was published.

I really believed the book would do well. The audiences prior to 1999 had connected with the material and it had proved useful to them in their job searches. We received several notes from audience members telling us how they used the lectures to land their first jobs. I still have several of these notes today. I thought the book would be a "no brainer."

Boy, was I wrong! While the book did OK, selling out of its first printing, it was not a big success. At the time we chalked it up to my writing skills, or lack of them! Or maybe the topic was better for lectures than the written word. Those things may have been true, but we learned a decade later that the book was researched on one generation (Gen X) and written for another generation (Gen Y). In 1999 the first class of Gen Y graduated from college. I did not notice or understand this shift for nearly a decade.

As previously mentioned, in 2009 *Gen Y Now* was published. *Gen Y Now* was written for managers and leaders from the Baby Boomer and Gen X generations and was designed to help them attract and retain Gen Y employees. It was in doing the research for this book that I realized why my first book missed the mark. It was also during this time that I came to understand the major demographic shift that was occurring, which has lead to the book you are now reading.

Unlike our failure to read the signs and understand the demographic shift in 1999, we do not want experienced professionals like yourself to read the current evidence a decade too late. Peter Drucker (author of dozens of business books and the man who invented the term management consultant) said that demographic shifts are a major factor that you can predict with complete accuracy. The current change is what I want you to understand at a core level because it will impact your consulting for decades. There are four key shifts you should consider as you think about starting your own consulting practice:

1) Demographics

2) The new math

3) The new normal

4) Profiting from past mistakes

Each of these shifts is evidence as to why being an independent consultant is a very logical career choice at this time. Also, each of these shifts presents enormous opportunities for you to help organizations with the new reality if you choose this career path.

Four Key Shifts That Make Consulting a Real Opportunity

Key shift #1:
Demographics

The biggest cultural shift today is the age and characteristics of workers and managers (demographics). This shift influences your ability to get a "regular" job, the kinds of people you'll work with, and the kind of consulting that is in demand. When we started to write *Gen Y Now,* it quickly became apparent why this generation is able to effect so much change in society and the work world. Like Boomers before them, it was pure numbers first. Gen Y will put their stamp on our future and there is nothing that can stop them. They are the majority generation at this time, and will be for quite some time.

GENERATION	BORN	NUMBER
Baby Boomers	1946–1964	77.7 million
Generation X	1965–1976	48.0 million
Generation Y	1977–1995	79.5 million

The baby boom began in 1946 and continued until 1964. During that time 77.7 million Boomers were born in the United States. As mentioned earlier, on January 1, 2011, the first Baby Boomer turned 65, and a Baby Boomer will continue to turn 65 every 8.5 seconds until 2029. This huge generation is marching toward retirement at a record pace.

Generation X followed the Boomers. From 1965 until 1976 there were 48 million X'ers born. Given all of the research we have done, we still do not know why their time frame was shorter, though we have uncovered several possible reasons, from technology defining the groups to birth rates. While there is some variation in how people count the generations, the table shows the most accepted years and numbers for them .

Beginning in 1977, Gen Y continued until 1995. These individuals are the first "technology natives" ever and they are 79.5 million strong. Gen Y is larger than the Boomer generation by a couple of million and significantly larger than Gen X.

Purely on the basis of numbers, it is a statistical certainty that the future of work will be defined by Gen Y. Their "native" status, growing up with technology, gives them an edge, even over Gen X which is fairly tech savvy.

As it relates to numbers in the workforce, if we look at the generations moving forward, for the next 18 years Gen Y will grow even larger as compared to the other generations. By 2029 the youngest Boomer will be 65 while the youngest X'er will be 53 and the youngest Y'er will be 34.

USING DEMOGRAPHIC SHIFTS

It is important to understand these demographic shifts as you consider hanging out your own shingle. The quicker you understand Gen Y and develop an appropriate strategy, the quicker you can succeed in this new reality. What I am seeing is too many people being like I was in 1999 when I wrote my first book. Too many people are not reading the signs and are developing a consulting or job search strategy for a market that no longer exists.

It's interesting how all that you've done can come together to create new opportunities. For me, it was the book to help students get jobs, our work on Generation Y, my sales experience and my consulting career. For you, it might be your past experience and the information in this book that will help you build a new career. It is a drastic mistake for Baby Boomers to base their future job plans on the past economy. The market has changed dramatically. Doors are closing but new opportunities are opening in turn.

In the last major downturn in 2001, the oldest Boomer was only 55. These experienced folks still had at least a decade of work life ahead of them based upon the traditional retirement age. In 2001 the oldest X'er was only 36, and the oldest Y'er was just out of college, at 24.

When the economy picked back up following 9/11, businesses needed the experience and leadership that could only be gained by hiring back Baby Boomers. Gen X'ers, while experienced, did not have enough critical mass to replace the Boomers. In 2001, Gen Y'ers were simply too young to be serious contenders to replace Boomer experience.

Fast forward. Today the situation is totally different. By 2012 the entire Gen X cohort was at least 36 years old and the oldest was 47. Also by 2012 over half of Gen Y was at least 26 years old. I am not being ageist, just pointing out the ages and the corresponding experience. Today there is plenty of talent available to replace Baby Boomers. I believe it is a mistake in your job search to ignore these facts. Too many folks have tried to find a job, leveraging their resumes and experience in a market that no longer exists, or at least in a market where other alternatives are available to the hiring organization and the odds are against you. People often think entrepreneurs are big risk takers. In fact, entrepreneurs like to stack the odds in their favor, and that's what I want to do for you.

What IS missing for the hiring organization, and why independent consultants have an enormous opportunity, is knowledge-transfer strategies. To be blunt, most businesses do not have a knowledge-transfer strategy and have not taken the time to document and leverage their experienced workers' knowledge. When experienced workers left during the recession, the company also lost the knowledge capital of those workers. There may be many hiring alternatives for organizations to replace workers, but there are not too many alternatives for companies to replace their lost knowledge.

While companies may not want to hire a 20-, 30-, or 40-year experienced professional full time, there is no doubt they need their knowledge capital. They just don't want to pay "full freight." Business leaders are much more willing to add variable costs versus fixed cost to their profit-and-loss statements. The economic downturn has taught them to stay nimble. Fixed expenses are an anchor. Variable costs, such as consultant expenses, allow businesses to achieve results while not "weighing down" their financials with long-term employee costs. You are a variable cost when you consult.

The Knowledge-Capital Bank

When companies have a pool of experience, it's like money in the bank. It provides a sense of security and confidence. For years business owners watched their people's wealth of knowledge grow. This knowledge was there when new hires needed to draw upon it, when new circumstances required it or when emergencies came up. Now a great deal of this knowledge capital is gone, leaving soon, or just plain disengaged. Businesses will need to find a way to make deposits back into their "Knowledge Capital Bank" without adding to fixed costs.

Key shift #2:
The new math

As businesses try to figure out how to grow the top and bottom lines, there is still a major focus on the middle line, expenses. For most organizations salary and benefits continue to be their single largest expense. Organizations are trying to prosper by managing costs.

Business owners are also very aware that they may have achieved the maximum productivity gains possible from their remaining workforces. Folks have been forced to do more with less for quite some time now. There is little room in the margins for the remaining workers to tackle important new projects and strategies, let alone improve ongoing operations.

We are seeing business leaders coming to grips with this conundrum. They want to initiate projects to grow their businesses or streamline their operations, but they do not have the bandwidth to get it done. They know that in order to succeed they need to do it, but they will not hire additional employees to achieve it. Spending too much on additional employees may doom them in the short term, yet failing to invest may doom them in the long run. In addition, the people who are still on staff may not have the requisite experience, time, or knowledge to tackle special, innovative, and strategic issues.

Business leaders who have survived the downturn are more convinced than ever that the answer to their project and strategic needs is *not* adding people to the payroll. Gains in productivity and the advancement of technology have allowed businesses to survive. This is one of the major reasons economists cite the "jobless" recovery. For years economists have called 4.5% unemployment "full employment." Now there is reason to believe that the voting public will accept a much higher number moving forward.

This brings us to the new math. For example, if an employer has a need for additional employees and a budget of, say, $150,000, they have a few choices. They could go out and hire a 30-year professional and spend the entire $150K. This might give them the knowledge capital they need, but not necessarily all of the manpower to accomplish the job. PLUS, with salary and benefits totaling $150k, this new hire may even feel UNDERcompensated based upon previous levels of income.

Option two is to hire two, or even three, young employees. You may get technical knowledge but little industry knowledge. You may get enthusiasm but add to your training costs as the new hires take time to come up to speed. You will get the manpower but not necessarily the strategic understanding to drive the projects.

Option three is to spend the money a bit differently. It is this option that is an enormous opportunity for independent consultants. A business owner could hire TWO folks for $50,000 each AND hire an experienced consultant for $40,000 and SAVE $10,000! This situation gives a business owner the best of all worlds. In this scenario there would be enough manpower to accomplish tasks, and enough knowledge capital to direct strategic thinking and drive solutions. PLUS, in this scenario, the business owner would also have young talent on board for future growth. And you can add to this the fact that a knowledge transfer would be taking place from the consultant to the staff. Gen Y particularly likes opportunities to learn so they would prefer being under the mentorship of an experienced consultant. A true win, win, win situation.

Our experience tells us that the market is very open to hiring top talent on a project basis. We also know that during the recession many businesses put strategic initiatives on the back burner, and now is the time they are willing to tackle these issues. One of the laws of consulting we have learned over these past many years is this: Once business owners have decided to tackle these initiatives that were on hold they want them done YESTERDAY! This sense of urgency provides a major opportunity for independent consultants.

In addition to the opportunities that are being presented by established businesses, there are also a record number of start-up companies who could use your help. A well-funded start up often looks to a consultant for early guidance that becomes ongoing counsel.

Key shift #3:
The new normal

The only constant is change. How many times have you heard that line? Maybe as a leader you even told it to your team. It sure is easier to understand and embrace when the change is affecting someone else! When the change affects us, it seems less logical and much more emotional.

The Harvard Business Review (*HBR*) regularly highlights what they think is the next "big idea." In May 2012, *HBR* published an article, "The Rise of the Supertemp." This article used the term "supertemp" and we use the term "solopreneur."

HBR says supertemps (solopreneurs) are "increasingly trusted by corporations to do mission critical work that in the past would have been done by permanent employees or established firms." The article goes on to state that these independent consultants "are growing in number, and we think they're on the verge of changing how businesses work."

While there are certainly opportunities in the *Fortune* 500 for independent consultants, consulting is by no means just for large corporations. Since we started our firm we have worked for several dozen *Fortune* 500 companies, but our "bread and butter" is in small- to medium-sized firms. These firms are anxious to acquire the knowledge and experience needed to formulate and execute strategic initiatives.

In the United States alone, there are nearly 200,000 middle market businesses ($10 million – $1 billion in revenue) and over 24 million small businesses (under $10 million in revenue). This is a huge market for your services and experience as an independent consultant. There is also a large international market. By leveraging technology you can service clients around the world almost as easily as those in North America.

Several years ago Spencer Johnson wrote *Who Moved My Cheese?* It rose to the top of the best seller lists in no time. It was a simple parable about two mice, Hem and Haw. Haw was the character who adapted quickly to change and Hem did not. If you have not read this book, I would highly recommend it. (It takes less than an hour to read.)

The question for you is quite simple. Which character are you? Are you adapting to change or are you hesitating? Are you like I was in writing my first book and not reading the signs, or are you looking at the statistical facts and drawing strategic conclusions? Are you using the data to make informed career choices, or are you hoping the cheese will be where it always was?

There is a new normal in our workforce, competitive arena, technology, and even management. Looking at this data in conjunction with the demographic and new-math points made above will help you realize that leveraging your knowledge and experience to become an independent consultant may be the most lucrative and enjoyable decision of your career (more on this in later chapters).

NEW NORMAL OPPORTUNITY #1:
START UPS
The latest available data shows that in 2009 business start ups reached their highest level since the tech boom of 1999 and this trend to entrepreneurship continues. Millions of folks believe the best answer to their career ambitions lies in their own efforts. As many as 20% of the population would like to be in their own businesses. Many folks are starting companies

from scratch and there have been a record number of people buying franchises. This poses two very distinct opportunities for independent consultants.

The first opportunity is the growing market for your knowledge and experience. As new entrepreneurs are getting started, they will need your insights along the way. These entrepreneurs will not be able to "afford" a resume like yours, but may be quite willing to invest in your ability as a consultant to drive results and to front end their success. The "new math" will be of particular interest to this group.

These new entrepreneurs span all of the generations. There are Baby Boomers who by choice or need have ventured out on their own, as well as individuals from Gen X and Gen Y. Each of these cohorts will have the need, for very different reasons, to connect with experienced professionals who can offer advice, counsel, and additional bandwidth. Your knowledge capital will be highly desirable to these new business owners.

The second opportunity for you as an independent consultant is to become your own boss, one of the new entrepreneurs, if you will, without the major investment that most franchises and other businesses require. Our research shows that most viable franchises cost a good deal up front and as much as $500–$22,000 a month in residual fees. A February 27, 2012 article in *Forbes* magazine rated the best franchises for the money. The average cost to start a franchise was $135K (Snap-on), $293K (7-Eleven), $420K (Aaron's), $1.447 million (Panera Bread), $156K (Servpro), $1.480 million (McDonald's), $63K (Liberty Tax Service), $66K (Merry Maids), $106K (The Maids International), and $395K (Jimmy John's). These investments are significant. Many of these franchises are counting on your work ethic and business acumen, combined with their processes and brand, to provide a winning formula. While I think I could run many of these franchises, they don't look that good to me compared to consulting.

To become an independent consultant, the cost of entry is MUCH less. In fact, your investment to get started will be less than some franchises' *monthly* residual fees. Your success is also based upon your work ethic and business acumen. The difference is what you need to get started, which is far less than any "brick-and-mortar" business.

NEW NORMAL OPPORTUNITY #2:
TIMING AND MOMENTUM

There is a significant reason you should be looking at the unemployment figures in making your decision to become an independent consultant. Like anything you have ever done in your career, you will only get better at consulting as you gain experience. The sooner you get started, the sooner you will become comfortable and more expert.

Over the next several years hundreds of thousands of people will try to become independent consultants. The issue is not that competition will grow. We believe there is more than enough demand to meet the supply, and we have a deep belief in an abundance mentality. The issue is in the types of engagements you will receive, your ability to create long-term relationships, and the scalability and the profitability of your engagements. The sooner you start, the more time you'll have to build the type of business you want.

We believe those folks who start working on their new craft now will have a better chance of securing engagements that will create long-term relationships. Our experience has proven this out. The more results we have provided, the more we have created almost evangelical referrals and references for later business. Business owners will have these types of strategic needs for the next few years and will create long-term relationships with those folks who have helped them at this time.

I'm enthusiastic about consulting. It's been very good to me, both financially and in doing work I like. But to succeed you need to be someone who gets things done, and this generally takes a positive or aggressive attitude. For example, I know two brothers, both of whom are very smart. When presented with a challenge, the first brother thinks, "If anyone can do it, I can.

And if I don't know something that's required to do the job, I can find out." The second brother's mind automatically goes to the problems with a project: "What about the possibility of getting sued? What if I fail? What if things take too long?" And so on. Unless you are a risk consultant, a lawyer, an insurance consultant, or possibly an accountant, this attitude will *not* make you a successful consultant. (And, in fact, the first brother is an entrepreneur while the second brother has worked successfully for nonprofits and is a *great* employee.)

You must have a can-do attitude and project quiet confidence to prospects and clients even when you're not sure how you'll solve a problem. Your skill should be in finding solutions, not in having all the answers. The key is having the confidence to know you will find a solution.

Here are some key facts to consider that show the benefits of acting like Haw (the decisive mouse in *Who Moved My Cheese?*), and not Hem.

- In a recent *USA Today* survey of 27 prominent economists, 23 believed that unemployment will return to 5% but only 3 think it will be before 2015! Some economists believe unemployment won't get lower than 6% before 2020.

- In January 2011 the US Department of Labor statistics changed its process for recording how long people have been unemployed. The old norm was two years and now it is five years.

- As already mentioned, in January 2011 the first Baby Boomers turned 65 and many will retire from their current positions. This will create a "knowledge vacuum" that can be filled by independent consultants.

- Many unemployed professionals are accepting underemployment in jobs that use their knowledge capital for significantly lower annual salaries.

- A survey conducted by MBO Partners in 2011 found that 80% of independent workers are satisfied with their situation. This number includes 58% who are highly satisfied.

The nature and makeup of the workforce has changed forever. In 1942 economist Joseph Schumpeter coined the phrase "creative destruction." He believed that capitalism, by its very nature reinvents itself constantly. This often involves the destruction of old technologies by new ones. If we were to just think about the past 10 years we would see his point. Who would have thought about Google, text messaging, "Skyping," smart phones, and so on just a few short years ago? The nature of employment in our capitalist free market economy is reinventing itself…again.

Key shift #4:
Profiting from past mistakes

As the economy recovers, businesses are going to realize they have made a few major miscalculations and will rush to correct these errors. It has been my experience that this will happen quickly and dramatically. We have all seen how organizations react to miscalculations. There is a tendency to swing 180 degrees the other way. Think about Enron and Sarbanes Oxley. As a society and as a business community we tend to over adjust. This over adjustment will provide independent consultants with a wealth of opportunities.

The first miscalculation of business leaders is believing that new productivity gains will continue at the same level and can be driven by technology alone. But technology will have decreasing effects on productivity in the future. The biggest gains have already been realized. Further, employees are tired. Since the recession they have been asked to do more with less. Overtime, lost vacations, stress at home, and missed children's events have taken their toll. This is a recipe for disaster.

Since the recession, many experienced people have left their jobs and taken their know how with them. Business leaders have come to rely VERY HEAVILY on the remaining workforce and their knowledge of "where the bodies are buried." There is a great deal of evidence that these "put upon" workers will leave the first chance they get to obtain a more normal work schedule. In fact, it is this group who are contributing a great deal to the new entrepreneurs we discussed earlier. Many folks are simply quitting, or will quit at the first opportunity. This will be a "strike two" for existing organizations (the third strike is coming!). Strike one is the loss of experienced workers due to the recession. Strike two is the inevitable loss of current workers due to burn out.

Strike three is the failure to prepare for knowledge capital leaving. VERY few businesses, especially small to medium organizations, have a knowledge-transfer strategy. For some reason, most businesses believe their current workforce is going to live and work forever! No real effort is put in place to teach a new generation of workers how to get things done most effectively and efficiently.

Here is the most interesting and ironic part. The next generation of workers, Gen Y, is DYING for this knowledge transfer. Gen Y is constantly asking "what's next" and is looking to constantly learn new information and processes. If an organization doesn't have a system to transfer knowledge, then Gen Y will ALSO leave. This is a deadly combination for business owners, and a problem that independent consultants can solve.

Independent consultants have the wealth of knowledge that organizations need. This knowledge can be accessed without needing to pay full freight as mentioned earlier. Finally, Gen Y, in addition to wanting knowledge transfer, is ALSO DYING for mentors and leaders. Independent consultants can provide the "triple threat":

$$\begin{array}{l} \text{Knowledge capital} \\ +\ \text{Cost effectiveness} \\ \underline{+\ \text{Leadership}} \\ =\ \textbf{Demand for your skills} \end{array}$$

If you're a talented Baby Boomer sitting on the sidelines at the moment, or not fulfilled with your current job, you might want to consider hanging up your own shingle. You may want to decide if this is the time to become a consultant. Experienced professionals can relatively quickly become successful consultants by packaging their wealth of knowledge and finding five or ten places where they can offer their skills. I know that it can be done. I also know that organizations are dying to have access to this wealth of knowledge and that five or ten assignments will add up to a higher income than any single job.

Summary

There is a loss of knowledge capital happening to companies as Baby Boomers retire. This means that:

- Companies need your experience but don't want to create the fixed cost of full-time, experienced employees; and

- Gen Y employees can do the work, but need mentors to get up to full speed.

Take those two factors together and it's clear that many companies could benefit from your expertise in the role of consultant.

I love the consulting career and think that many other professionals can benefit from it. In this book I'll give you some points that may help you decide about the potential of consulting for you, as well as a few tips that can help you be successful. As I mentioned earlier, there's lots of work for all of us, and I'd like to have more skilled colleagues available as resources for our clients. I believe the overall economy will be positively impacted as we get our collective years of experience and knowledge "back in the game."

There are at least four forces converging to make now a great time to consider consulting as a career:

- Shifting demographics – Gen Y at 79.5 million strong are here to stay.
- The need of business owners to have more knowledge capital.
- The new math provides lucrative opportunities.
- Businesses do not want to add fixed costs but may take on variable costs.

CHAPTER 2

What It Takes to Succeed in Consulting

Up to this point I've talked mainly about the opportunities in consulting. What I'd like to discuss next is what you have to actually do to **SUCCEED** in consulting. You should know that hanging up your own shingle is hard work. None of the requirements to succeed are easy. You have to start and run a business and you have to sell your services. Just because you have the talent to help organizations doesn't mean they will hire you!

Before you can even get started you will need to figure out how to package your career experience in such a way that organizations will be interested. You have to establish your credibility and come across as competent and helpful. You do not need to have an exhaustive marketing plan. You simply have to know how your resume and experience can open doors. (More about that in Chapter 4.)

You need to do three major things to have a successful consulting business.

1. **You need to find clients.** You have to market and sell yourself. (This is the difficult

part of consulting for most people.) (See Chapter 4 on selling yourself.)

2. **You need to create solutions.** (See Chapter 6.)

3. **You need to deliver your solutions that drive results.** (See Chapter 7.)

Why would anyone in their right mind want to take on all this? Because it can be one of the most rewarding careers in the world. Even if the current trends did not point to consulting as a good career choice, being a consultant could very well be the biggest reward in itself. Consulting provides interesting challenges. You work with a variety of companies. And you have status and financial success. As an added bonus, what a consultant can do for the "greater good" is unbelievable.

A consultant has the opportunity to change lives for the better. When we have been successful, we have created jobs and increased job satisfaction. People are more productive, happier, and more engaged. Study after study shows that workers who are more engaged take a sense of pride home, and also have more productive out-of-work lives. In short, people can become better employees, husbands, wives, neighbors and community leaders as a direct result of *your* efforts. You may think I am exaggerating, but I am not. I really believe that this is a noble profession and that independent consultants do noble work.

So, are you Hem or Haw? Do you have the kind of "can-do" attitude that will take you to success? What do you need to challenge in your own belief system to make consulting work for you? (See also Chapter 8.)

World-Class Performers

During the past few years, my staff and I have spent countless hours researching world-class performers. We have interviewed dozens of people who perform at world-class levels including athletes, actors, musicians, politicians, and business executives. We found that they possess a common set of behaviors and skills. The same behaviors and skills can be learned and implemented by you to create a successful consulting practice.

1) Seek out a coach or mentor.
2) Use performance feedback.
3) Turn unconscious tendencies into conscious choices.
4) Realize that what is required for improvement may be counterintuitive.
5) Manage energy.
6) Develop actionable plans.

1. Seek out a coach or mentor

World-class performers look outside themselves to find a set of eyes that can give them advice and feedback to help them get better. They seek out somebody who is not necessarily better than them at a given task. They find folks who may not even be good at the task about which they're coaching. Instead, what they're good at is having a discerning eye. They're good at identifying a tendency that helps their mentees get better.

Let me give you an example using professional actors and actresses. We have interviewed several very successful people. Everyone we interviewed told us that they don't have to find an established "superstar" coach for a mentor. Their coaches don't have to have won Oscars or Emmys. What they have to find is someone who can provide them with that important set of outside eyes. The right mentor can help us understand our tendencies and what we may need to do to get better. In fact, most great acting coaches never actually made their living as an actor or actress, but each had a gift for coaching others.

2. Use performance feedback

All World-Class Performers use performance feedback. Actors and actresses film themselves and then look at what they've done. Musicians record themselves, and athletes have game film. They study performance feedback in order to understand what their tendencies are—those small, almost imperceptible things that may keep them from being the best of the best.

What kind of game film do you have? Go back through your career. Do you have any performance appraisals? Have you taken a 360-degree evaluation? What kind of feedback have you received along the way?

3. Turn unconscious tendencies into conscious choices

World-class performers realize that they have unconscious tendencies. These are things that they do because they've always done them. They realize that they need to turn these tendencies into conscious choices.

World-class performers understand that it's critical to stay in the moment. It is vital that they stay focused and not go on "auto-pilot." That's not to say that they don't have very highly tuned skills that allow them to do certain things without thought, but what they understand is that they need to stay in the moment and remain there.

4. Realize that what is required for improvement may be counterintuitive

World-class performers understand that what might be necessary for improvement can feel completely counterintuitive. Most people are able to drive a reasonable level of results because they leverage their natural talents well. World-class performers leverage their talents *and* learn that what might be critical for success may feel quite uncomfortable and not be at all natural.

If you want to be a world-class performer, you need to step up and understand that you don't know everything. You have to develop some unnatural, counterintuitive skill sets and get comfortable with new processes.

5. Manage energy

World-class performers learn that they have to manage their energy. We all know that we have 24 hours in a day. We wouldn't have gotten to the level of our careers that we've reached if we didn't understand how to prioritize or how to get things done. We know that there's only so much time in the day.

World-class performers also know that there's only so much gas in their gas tank every day. They know that they have to manage their energy judiciously— just like their time. They understand that they can't waste their energy on unproductive activities. This concept is going to be very important as you develop your consulting practice. Don't waste your energy on people or tasks that do not help you move your business along.

6. Develop an actionable plan

World-class performers create an actionable plan. They understand their strengths and build upon them. Having a coach and studying performance feedback helps. In addition to building upon their strengths, all world-class performers seek to uncover their blind spots. They do not want to be derailed by something they are completely unaware of. The want to know their weak areas. They do not waste time on being defensive. All world-class performers set about minimizing their blind spots and maximizing their strengths. With this knowledge they then develop a plan.

The plans of the world-class performers we interviewed tended to have the following traits:

- The actions need to be countable. Did you do it or didn't you do it?

- The plans were not overwhelming. You need to "eat the elephant one bite at a time."

- The plans were written. Writing it down is critical because then it becomes more real.

- The plans were communicated. Share your plan with someone. It can be a friend, your coach, or your mentor.

- Adapt, adapt, adapt. A plan will constantly provide you with data points. Your job is to adapt your behaviors to the data in order to maximze your success.

Counterintuitive World-Class Success Traits for Consultants

People will continue to do what has worked in the past or what they intuitively think will work. They fail to challenge their own assumptions. As mentioned above, in our work with world-class performers, one of the universal things we uncovered is that world-class performers are willing to challenge their intuitions and do things that are "counterintuitive" in order to succeed.

Different circumstances require different actions. The truly world-class performers realize this and adapt

How New Consultants Lose Confidence

One of the problems we see new consultants experiencing is what we call the "confidence slide." This slide involves four steps:

Step #1. The technique or action does not work so instead of adapting; we just do it more often and even harder, causing stress and lost energy.

Step #2. Our failure to adapt and our heightened stress is met with resistance from our intended audience and the message is interpreted by us as "they aren't getting it" instead of "we aren't getting it."

Step #3. We then begin to judge our audience as "stupid" or "against us" and blame them for our failure.

Step #4. We do not understand why we are failing and begin to take it personally, allowing our confidence to slide away.

In order to break this slide we need to have a mechanism to challenge each step along the process, so any fix is process related (adapting) and not personal (lost confidence).

accordingly. There are five areas where new consultants need to be counterintuitive to succeed. What may have been "natural" work habits and beliefs in the past now need to be challenged in the face of a new reality.

Counterintuitive challenge #1:
The work world has changed forever

The nature of work and skills needed by employers will be dramatically different moving forward. Employers will look for more "just-in-time" talent to address their business challenges. The recession has taught business owners that there is no need to carry certain skill sets on their payroll full time. Expertise can be acquired on an as-needed basis. Teams of experienced experts can be formed almost instantly. Information can be shared by each team member quickly with no geographical barriers. These teams can be assembled and disassembled anytime, anywhere, to tackle any challenge. Once the result is achieved, there is no residual expense for the business.

"There is a tendency for mid-career individuals to think very linearly," says author and speaker Shawn Graham. (Shawn is a frequent contributor/writer in *Fast Company* magazine.) "In the old paradigm when someone was looking for a job, they packaged a resume, left 'Job A' and found 'Job B.' It usually was a one-for-one replacement. In fact, often times it was a one-for-one replacement in the same field or profession. For example, if someone worked in health care, their next job was also in health care. Now people should be looking to trade Job A for project B, C, D, and E."

Graham believes there are several forces contributing to this shift. "The recent recession certainly contributed to this whole shift," says Graham. "However, that is just one part of the equation. There are two other key areas to consider. People who retained their employment during the downturn may well come out of the recession 'burned out' or just plain fearful of losing their job the next time. Many of these folks are more than willing to take control of their careers and start something on their own."

"When you add Gen Y to this list, 79 million strong, you have a 'sea change' occurring," emphasizes Graham. "Gen Y may be the most educated generation of all time and has embraced the shift towards jobs and careers that have a meaning and a purpose beyond financial. This group of young professionals is very motivated to hang up their own entrepreneurial shingles." I would add that even when Gen Y takes a job or series of jobs, they want to be in control of their own careers. They don't just want jobs, they want to do something meaningful or learn new skills for their portfolios.

All indications are that the labor supply will continue to outpace demand for full time jobs in the near future. Not wanting to add to payroll, business owners will **DEMAND** just-in-time talent and, because of the shift in workers' attitudes, the supply will be readily available. This shift will make it even more difficult for mid-career professionals to land traditional jobs.

In the next chapter we will dig more into how independent consultants should package their experience. Our research – and our experience – proves that mid-career professionals don't always know what all they know.

Counterintuitive challenge #2:
Location independence is now a reality

When most Baby Boomers, and Gen X'ers for that matter, started their careers, working "virtually" was as far-fetched as some of the contraptions on "Star Trek." Having laptops, hand-held communication devices, Bluetooth headsets, video phones, and access to a worldwide communication system like the Internet was only available in the Jetson's world. Now, a simple hand-held device can keep a professional linked to others around the world 24/7.

Baby Boomer and Gen X careers started in the "to be working you must be present in the office" era. Many Boomers prided themselves on being the first into the office and the last to leave. The bosses noticed. If someone was in early and out late they were considered a "hard worker." Simply being there meant you were working hard. Early in and late out was rewarded. Boomers and X'ers were rewarded for their time commitment.

"When I started coaching, there was no one who put in more time than me" said basketball coach of the year, Herb Sendek. "I prided myself on my time commitment. In fact, I chuckle now when I think back to those days at Providence. I would have been embarrassed if Coach Pitino had beaten me into the office. Sometimes he would call me early in the morning and I now wonder if he was just checking on me to see if I was crazy enough to be there that early. At the time I took his calls to be a validation of my work ethic."

"Things now are dramatically different" says Sendek. "Coaches can be anywhere and have access to everything they need to get the job done. Databases, films, documents – everything can be accessed remotely. I have had to come to grips with this reality. I do not have to see my coaches to know they are working. Also, and maybe more importantly, this change has allowed a degree of improvement for our coaches' family lives. This is a 24/7 profession and having access beyond the office gives one the ability to tuck their children in at night."

Counterintuitive challenge #3: Collaboration is king

Having worked with several colleges and universities there has been a very important shift over the years in how students are taught and how they are required to complete assignments. In the '70s, '80s, and early '90s, students were very much on their own. Curriculums emphasized individual performance and classes and grades were highly competitive.

What businesses learned from this was that the students they were hiring were very well-versed on the technical aspects but lacked the social and communication skills necessary to get their points across and work on teams and in work groups. Chris Martin, vice president for university relations at West Virginia University, observes that "students in the late '80s and early '90s were more cynical, distrustful and 'lone wolf' types. They didn't always work well in groups. Today's students are joiners and they are more community-oriented. It was harder in the '80s to get students to join classroom communities. Today it is much easier."

One of the big things the Internet has done is develop communities. In 2010, Mark Zuckerberg, founder of Facebook, was *Time* magazine's person of the year. Facebook's community has over 900 million users. Regardless of what anyone thinks of this technology or its uses, the fact remains it is here, and here to stay.

Many mid-career professionals find this need to collaborate difficult. Shawn Graham points out that "not that long ago Richard Florida wrote a best seller *The Rise of the Creative Class*. Now, creativity is a given.

There is a movement now towards a 'collaborative class.' People are searching for ways to leverage technology and develop meaningful connections. Virtual affinity groups and communities are a treasure trove of information."

Technology has certainly made it much easier to connect to others and collaborate on an unprecedented scale. However, Graham believes, "The primary driver behind what is taking place has been the need to fill education gaps. Niche groups can form and provide targeted information that might otherwise be ignored or overlooked."

You may need to battle your old, "intuitive" self and realize that being a lone wolf may no longer be the best strategy.

Counterintuitive challenge #4:
We may be prejudiced against certain technologies

Speaking personally, I originally believed Facebook was invented for college students to post inappropriate photos and create a digital legacy that would embarrass them in the future, if not ruin their lives! It should be noted, I felt that way in spite of the fact that I am a nationally recognized advocate for Gen Y!

To be frank, I am not so sure my original thoughts were all that wrong THEN...however, that was then and this is now.

Technology, and in particular, collaboration tools, have advanced to the point of being "must haves" in a business's arsenal. If you are carrying any prejudice about these tools, as I did, now is the time to get over it. In fact, these tools will give you a competitive edge when working with clients. On consulting engagements we are using "cloud applications" internally and externally with our clients. Our clients are able to understand in real time what is happening on their projects and see the results as milestones are completed.

This is a challenge that some mid-career folks need to tackle, myself included; a hesitancy to embrace technology. We started our careers without most of the tools now used, and if you have not been active in the workplace in the past 6–12 months, there are even newer tools being used. We often hear the terms "digital native" referring to Gen Y and "digital immigrants" referring to Gen X and Boomers who have had to play catch up with online tools. We have found that many Boomers and X'ers may UNNECESSARILY lack confidence when it comes to embracing new tools.

Andrew Wood, author of *Making It Big in America* and a series of *Cunningly Clever Entrepreneur* books, says that "Baby Boomers worry too much about how hard learning new tech skills is. It's easy to understand the concepts involved and familiarity with them comes with a little practice." For example, we know a seventy-three-year-old sales consultant, Jack Sweeney, who is seldom in the office or at home and happily conducts his whole life on his iPhone.

Counterintuitive challenge #5: Employers do not want 100% of your time—they want results

The reality is that professionals earning six-figure incomes working in corporate America are being paid handsomely for only 10–20% of their productive time.

If you (or someone you know) ever worked in corporate America and earned $100,000 plus, stop and think (or ask someone) how your schedule looked from day to day, week to week, month to month and year to year. Was your time filled with high-level strategic activities 100% of the time? Were all of your efforts spent on driving core initiatives or, more likely, were there lots of useless meetings, wasted projects, and needless paperwork? My bet is that much more time was wasted than was productive!

John Kella, owner of JR Kella & Associates, started a consulting practice after spending months looking for the next "right opportunity." He began to realize consulting was his best choice. "It is unbelievable how productive you can really be when unencumbered with useless meetings and bureaucracy," says Kella.

"I have always been lucky enough to work for good companies," continues Kella, "so I did not waste too much time on needless politics and back biting.

However, many of the folks I have met were not so lucky! Even for me, in a great situation, nearly half of my time was spent on unproductive tasks. If you add in politics and in-fighting, I would guess that number could be as high as 70–75% of unproductive time."

Kella believes that less than 10% of his time now is wasted on non-core activities. "As an independent consultant, I can really focus my time and energy on producing results for a client and not working off of someone else's agenda. Because of that I can maintain several clients at one time."

When consultants accept that we are trading "Job A" for "Projects B, C, D, and E" we must also accept the reasons we are hired for these projects. Those reasons are simple. First, when an organization wants to get something new done, it can be extremely costly. Everyone in the organization is already busy with a job or they wouldn't be there! As outsiders, we have the expertise and experience to take on new tasks and accomplish the organization's goal. We are being hired as independent consultants to cut through the waste and spend our time and talents on the top 20% of the most important things needed to drive results. This is why the "new math" works. Clients hire consultants to bring just-in-time manpower and knowledge to solve critical business issues. Here is the key to profits and success for you: To leverage 20% of your knowledge and experience WILL NOT TAKE 100% of your time!

You know what you know, and have done what you have done. You have not gotten to this point without major accomplishments and being a problem-solver. David Maloney, former vice president of development

Entry into the
Consulting Field

PAST BARRIERS
Not enough skilled professionals available to tackle large projects.

CURRENT SITUATION
A wealth of experience available in almost all fields, much of it remotely via the Internet.

Large investment in technology hardware and software required to run a business.

Low-cost cloud applications and hardware.

Required marketing investment too large to "get known."

Free Internet-based tools and techniques.

Office staff for support, printing and shipping.

Freelance assistants available including online, Fedex, Kinkos, and so forth.

Networking groups = job seekers.

Networking groups = fellow consultants/ support.

for Oklahoma University, retired and discovered there was a demand for his knowledge capital as a consultant. He and I had several conversations about him becoming an independent consultant. While he wanted to help others and earn income, he didn't want to "work 60-hour weeks" again. We talked at length about how to price his services, how to not trade time for money, and how to leverage his years of experience to help others (and himself.) Dave quickly had enough clients to satisfy his schedule and income goals. During a follow-up conversation, Dave said with a chuckle, "I didn't realize I knew so much. I didn't know I was that smart." Maloney continued, "I'm just telling people what I know and how to get it done. I don't have to be in their offices eight hours a day. I just have to help them get their results. After all of these years, I guess I did learn something."

You are a resource loaded with solutions. Maybe the first time you accomplished a given task it took a significant percentage of your time, but now you know what you know. The trick is pulling what you know out of your head and marketing it to several clients. In the next chapter we will discuss this in more detail.

Summary

Hanging up your own shingle will be hard work. In order to maximize your success you can follow what world-class performers do to succeed. One of the big things all world-class performers do is realize that what might be necessary to succeed may well not come naturally to them. It may be completely counterintuitive. As an independent consultant, you need to realize the work world has changed forever. Location independence is a reality. COLLABORATION IS KING. You may be prejudiced against certain technologies and believe people will only pay you for 100% of your time.

The truth is location independence, collaboration and technology are an independent consultant's best friends. Your clients want results, not 100% of your time. Being a consultant can be easier and more fun than being stuck in one organization with busy work and corporate politics.

CHAPTER 3

Building a Foundation for Success

Becoming an independent consultant can have many rewards. However, one benefit you will not hear from me is "life style." While it is true that you will be your own boss and manage your own time, you may find you really do not have much "free time." I am not saying – and will never say – that becoming an independent consultant is easy. In fact, it's quite the opposite. Getting started can be very hard and will require you to learn new things, discover new tools, and challenge yourself (and your clients) in ways that may make you uncomfortable.

What you will hear me say – and admittedly I am prejudiced – is that consulting can be extremely fulfilling. You have spent many years building competencies that can be applied to this new career. You have challenged yourself over the years, learned new skills, solved seemingly unsolvable problems and driven results for your employer(s) that far exceeded their expectations. You have achieved a great deal. Consulting is a way for you to leverage your skills and reap the rewards.

Sell Value, NOT Time

Clients often think they're buying your TIME. If you fill in as a freelancer when they have overflow work, that may be what you're selling. However, the better cases I want to deal with are when they want your knowledge capital, not your time. You are not being hired to punch a time clock. You are being hired to drive a result. If you can achieve that result in one week or one year, the VALUE to the client is the same, and your fee should reflect the result, not the time.

When Solutions 21 was getting started I met with someone who put the idea of selling value rather than time completely into perspective for me. He was in institutional development, meaning he raised money for colleges and universities. He gave me an overview of what he did and then told me a story.

His analogy for his business was, and I am para-phrasing, "Let's say I choose to charge some astro-nomical fee for my services. For example's sake, let's say I charge hourly. I don't really care what kind of hourly fee you want to use – $500 or $1,000 an hour, it really doesn't matter. Let's say, for this example we make it $500 and hour. A client calls me from the west coast (his offices were on the east coast) and asks me to come to a meeting the next day in Los Angeles. I fly out that night and attend the meeting first thing in the morning. After two hours of hearing about the challenge, I have an answer. I have been doing this for 30 years, and this particular answer has worked in the exact same situation in other locations. I tell them the solution, take the next hour and develop the implementation. My answer is going to mean $10,000,000 to their bottom line.

"Now, what is my bill? Do I bill them $1,500 for the 3 hours in the meeting? Do I bill them $7,000 for the flight time out and back plus the cost of the meeting? What did they really buy? Did they by my time, or did they buy a $10 million dollar solution and my 30 years of research and development?"

After he posed the above questions to me, he then told me a "consulting" story. I have heard it since and you may have heard it in one form or another as well.

A building owner has steam heat in his building. One VERY cold winter day the boiler goes out and the heat shuts down. In a bit of a panic the owner calls the local plumber, who has a reputation for knowing boilers. The plumber shows up and immediately heads to the basement boiler room. The owner is right on his heels, following him to the boiler room.

The plumber looks up and down the system taking everything in. He spends a few moments making sure of his solution and then pulls out a ball peen hammer. He walks over to a valve on the boiler and gives it three taps of the hammer. The boiler immediately starts back up pushing out heat.

The building owner is overjoyed! A crisis has been diverted! PLUS the plumber was only there for 15 minutes. The owner asks the plumber for his bill and the plumber hands it to him. The owner looks and is in shock...$300! He is livid! In fact, at this price the plumber would bill $1,200 an hour! He demands the bill be itemized.

The plumber shrugs his shoulders and takes the bill out of the owner's hands and writes "15 minutes onsite - $25, knowing where to tap the valve - $275."

My early mentor then asked me "What did the building owner buy? Did he buy a crisis diverted? Did he buy a working boiler? Did he buy heat? Did he buy 30 years of research and development? Or did he buy 15 minutes? This is a key lesson about structuring your work and billing for it. Until you're confident in billing for value, your clients may be like the building owner and question your fees for 'working such a short time.'"

Clients buy SOLUTIONS. Clients buy RESULTS. An independent consultant should never trade time for money. Clients are buying your know-how and your ability to get results. If you are simply trading time for money, at some point you will be faced with a very difficult ethical dilemma. If you find the solution to a client's problem in a short period of time, and you know it can be communicated, accepted and implemented in a quickly, will you give the answer and lose a wonderful billing opportunity, or will you take your time presenting the fix and bill more money? Should the plumber have "pretended" to work longer on the boiler, extending the amount of time the building was without heat, or should he have fixed it as quickly as possible and avoided the inevitable "frozen pipe" disaster?

These two stories helped me realize that clients are buying brain power, solutions, and the RESULTS you can achieve. Plus, as previously discussed, clients are buying the 20% of your brain they really need. You need to charge for value and results delivered, not time.

Enjoying the Variety in Consulting

Consulting can give you a chance to do very mean-ingful work in a variety of situations. Studs Terkel, in his book *Working,* talked about "mind numbing" work. Consulting is anything but mind numbing – actually just the opposite. You are hired to present solutions. You should enjoy rising to the challenge. It is critical you always "be on your game." You are there to help people.

In fact, one piece of advice we offer would-be con-sultants is if you do not want to be on your game all of the time, then consulting may not be for you. This is not a career choice for anyone who does not want to pro-duce results or be held accountable for their input and decisions. Slackers and bureaucrats need not apply. If you enjoy boring meeting and playing politics, get a job and hire consultants to do your real work!

Another rewarding aspect of consulting is the constant learning opportunities. Working with clients across so many diverse industries and around the world gives me the opportunity to acquire new knowledge. Not just about particular industries, but also about corporate and foreign cultures. We are able to see what works and what does not and cross-pollinate the best approaches.

Avoiding the Feast-or-Famine Trap

When Solutions 21 started in 1994 it did not take long to realize there was a "doom loop" (as author Jim Collins would say) for independent consultants. Early in our existence we met with several independent consultants and one theme continued to surface. There seemed to be a "feast or famine" situation for everyone.

Consultants told us, over and over again, that there seemed to be periods of intense work and then periods when no revenue was being generated. As I think back on those conversations I can remember the consultants blaming it on "the nature of the business." I believed it was one of the "truths" these folks held that, to be blunt, was simply not true. It was a self-fulfilling prophecy. These folks believed it, then it happened, therefore it must be true.

At any one time Solutions 21 may be servicing 50+ clients in five to ten countries. Even in the beginning when Solutions 21 was just starting out, we serviced

10 or 12 clients at any one time. We quickly found a way to break the cycle of "feast or famine."

Traditionally, other independent consultants would follow the three steps of 1) selling an engagement, 2) creating the solution for the client, and then 3) delivering that solution. Nothing happened until an engagement was sold and no one got paid until an engagement was delivered.

How all of this worked (and still works for folks following this model) was usually 90–100 days a year of actually getting paid and the rest working on the next possible engagement. During the "feast" times it seemed the consultants were jazzed because of the meaningful work and the nice paychecks. During the "famine" times several folks seemed borderline depressed. Also, we noticed that it got harder and harder for other consultants to find meaningful assignments following each intense delivery period. Many of the folks who were consulting in 1994 are no longer in business because of their inability to break this three-phase cycle.

Notice I said because of their inability to break the cycle, not because they were bad consultants. I am sure there were, and are, folks out there consulting who are not good consultants, but I am not referring to these people. I am referring to the folks who have great experience, great problem-solving skills, great communication skills, and innovative ideas. Many of these highly talented folks are not successful because of their limiting belief in the self-fulfilling prophecy of feast or famine.

Sell, Create, Deliver

Let's start with the last phase of the cycle: Delivery. This seems to be the most enjoyable part of the job for most consultants we know (followed by Creating and, lastly, Selling). After all, people became independent consultants in order to solve problems and leverage their past successes. It is logical, therefore, that most folks would enjoy the delivery portion of the business.

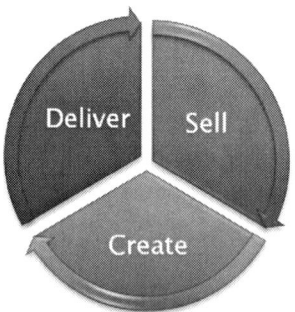

It is also logical that people tend to gravitate toward things they enjoy and are good at. Now, add to this the fact that consultants believe they only get paid when they are successfully delivering and you can see how someone could fool themselves that delivery is THE MOST IMPORTANT PART OF THE CYCLE. In fact, I strongly believe it is not. Each phase is important and all must be done well to be successful.

Scope creep

Let's look at what can happen if someone does not have a plan to attack the sales and creation phases of the cycle. The first problem is "scope creep." This is when the consultant takes on additional tasks for the client during a job that were not included in the original scope of work. After all, many consultants are billing themselves out hourly and the extra work is seen as additional revenue.

There are several problems with the decision to add tasks to a previously defined assignment. One of the biggest issues is trading time for money. If the consultant was selling solutions and results, instead of time, then portions of this scope creep could be additional very profitable projects. The other big problem with this is people are GIVING away the top 20% of their brain power. Let's go back to the plumber story. Let's say the plumber was there anyway, working on the restrooms, routine stuff with no real value-added. He is billing his usual $100 an hour when, suddenly, the heat goes out and the building owner panics. It is the coldest day of the year, the tenants are concerned, and the owner is worried about frozen pipes and angry tenants. This is a catastrophe in the making.

The owner runs to the plumber and asks for help. The plumber walks to the boiler room, taps the valve and goes back to the restroom to finish his work. This just gets added to his original bill and is just another part of his hourly rate. He fixed the boiler and avoided a major issue. But he only got paid for his time, not for the value he delivered.

I am not suggesting that you do not help clients avoid catastrophes when possible. This story is simply for illustration purposes. Seldom is there something we as consultants can do to "tap a valve" and fix a problem so quickly. My point is to not let this happen ALL OF THE TIME. If you are called into these situations REPEATEDLY then this is not just a "one off," it is scope creep. Fixing a major issue that is outside of your original scope is value added and you need to be recognized for providing this value. Doing it all of the time can be very damaging to your business.

TAPPING THE VALVE

Several years ago we were hired by a major metals manufacturer to re-engineer their order entry and delivery department. It seemed that over the years everyone had developed their own process for placing orders in the system and seeing that everything was delivered on time. Originally, there was a single process that everyone followed but over time it evolved into 10 or 12 different systems.

Our job was to study the best practices and develop one system to follow. In addition to the system design, we were also tasked with its implementation, which required a complete change-management strategy.

We sold our client on the value of working with us versus placing consultants there on an hourly basis. We were determined to champion our value-added and not trade time for money.

Within a day or two of us getting started we realized an enormous issue that could be fixed easily and bring in literally millions of dollars in extra revenue. Had we been trading time for money and not selling value we would have been faced with an ethical dilemma. Do we implement this fix right away and lose future billing opportunities, or do we do the right thing and tell the client? The fix was fairly simple and could be implemented almost immediately. Our client could be realizing millions of dollars of revenue in a short period of time.

I believe that no matter how we would have structured the proposal we would have done the right thing without hesitation. However, since we were selling our value and not time for money we were never faced with the ethical dilemma. We immediately told our client the fix and they were able to capitalize on the revenue opportunity the very next day.

Parkinson's Law

Now let's get back to the original premise that people tend to gravitate to work they enjoy and avoid work that is less enjoyable. We are also assuming most consultants do not have plans to attack the sales and (often) the creation phases of the cycle. With that in mind, let's look at what else can happen to derail a consultant's practice.

When there is no real plan to attack the other key areas of the consulting practice, and no time set aside to do so, people tend to become victims of "Parkinson's Law." Parkinson states that "work expands to fill the time available for its completion." For our purposes here this means that when consultants do not have a disciplined plan to work the sales and creation phases they will spend more time than is necessary on the part they like – on delivery of services. It is critical for you to understand that you need to pay attention to *all three* aspects of the business to be successful.

While few people know it today, Parkinson actually did a good deal of research to develop his "law." One example comes from the British navy during and after World War I:

Year	Ships	Men in Navy	Dockyard Workers	Dockyard Admin.	Navy Admin.
1914	62	146,000	57,000	3249	2000
1928	20	100,000	62,439	4558	3569
% Cg	-68%	-32%	+10%	+40%	+78%

After the war was over ships and men decreased as you'd expect, but support personnel increased, in some cases extravagantly! This is a major reason why large organizations need your help: They get less efficient with size.

While working for an organization, consultants tend to find additional fixes they can do for the organization that are outside the original scope of work. This is common and logical as they gain an inside view. But then they handle these things *while* they are on the current assignment. This adds value for the client, but if not managed appropriately is a major blow to the consultant. It tends to make these new insights simple add-ons that bill a few extra hours. If you were not trading time for money, but selling value and results,

Corrollaries to Parkinson's Law

While Parkinson's Law – that work expands to fill time available – is well known (from his book of the same name), he also had two related follow-up laws and books. His second law was that "Expenditure rises to meet income," and his third law was that "Expansion means complexity, and complexity decay." Until the publication of his best seller, *Parkinson's Law*, his work had been almost entirely on military and economic history. All his laws were intended to apply to large bureaucratic organizations, not small consulting firms. Thus, all his laws are yet another reason why large firms need your help as an outsider free of bureaucratic entanglements.

these additional "valves" would be additional opportu-nities. The truth of the matter is, if the consultant had SEVERAL other clients, and not just this single assign-ment, then turning these valves into opportunities would be more intuitive. The exchange of client results and consulting opportunity is a win/win proposition.

Energy Management

While talking to other consultants, I found early on that after completing an engagement they found it increas-ingly more difficult to find their next projects. It seemed to take longer and longer each time to find meaningful projects to tackle.

There are several reasons for this situation. First, many consultants need to "re-charge" following an intense client engagement. Since most independent consultants may not have a social community of peers to help with some of their problem-solving, they find themselves exhausted. For several weeks or months, they buried themselves in a project and poured all of their energy into the work.

It's fine to give your "all" to a client's needs, but you need a peer group to give you perspective and keep you grounded. It's hard to find peers in the con-sulting field who you can talk to frankly. Most are hus-tling up their next jobs, some are competitive with you, and so on. But, you need a sounding board, a group to cheer you on, and people to vent to and strategize with from time to time. Your goal should be to connect with (or create) a group of like-minded consultants who have an interest in your success.

Adding to the exhaustion that we saw in consultants, perhaps unconsciously, was the fact that they often didn't have another assignment on the horizon. The worry and stress of where the next engagement was coming from was in the back of their minds. Was the next sales and creation cycle going to be a long one? Would more work be there? How will they pay the bills?

Psychologically this feast-and-famine cycle can be a drain. After a great assignment and successful project, it is usually time to celebrate a job well done. Not having anywhere else to go following an engagement negates this feeling of satisfaction. The mind automatically worries about the future and spends little energy on celebration and reflection. This constant pressure can be draining.

Now you have a very talented consultant who just completed a very successful engagement, and they are tired and questioning themselves. In addition to this psychological hurdle that must be overcome to get a new assignment, there are two VERY real reasons most consultants find it hard to get the next assignment.

First, if you get completely caught up in the service-delivery phase, you are neglecting the sell-and-create phases. You need to be prospecting WITHIN your client as you deliver services. Your inside view should give you new insights and contacts that allow you to add new projects for that client.

Second, you may have made yourself irrelevant to other potential clients! Since all of your efforts have gone into one client, there has not been any activity with potential, future clients. That means starting from scratch...again. Instead, you should always budget some time to be in contact with other clients and prospects. If you don't, it means that anyone out there who could have benefited from your services while you were working on your current assignment has found another solution. They did not wait around for you. If business owners realize a challenge exists, often they want to work on it immediately. It is rare that business owners, given their tendency towards results and sense of urgency, will wait for a consultant's time to free up. Most likely, they will find another solution.

If an independent consultant spent weeks or months on a single engagement, it was not their imagination that the next assignment was harder to find. Many business owners who expressed interest in the past found another solution in the meantime. New prospects weren't being developed. Old prospects dried up. Folks needed to start from scratch at a time when their energy was zapped and their stress high. Getting caught up in the delivery cycle, trading time for money, versus maintaining several clients at once, and trading results for revenue, really is a "doom loop."

Your Natural Tendencies

Working backwards in the cycle from delivery, we need to look at the creation phase. Creating a solution for clients can be a great deal of fun.

One of the tools Solutions 21 has is an assessment that looks at a person's natural tendencies in the innovation process. Using this tool we learned there are many people – me included – who enjoy the creation portion of a task.

No matter what your preferred style is regarding the innovation cycle, you need to FIGHT YOUR NATURAL TENDENCIES. Your job as an independent consultant is to provide solutions that get results for the client. Your job as a business owner is to get results for yourself! All styles can suffer from the "law of diminishing returns." If you, as I do, love the creation of an idea and brainstorming, you need to know that you can over-create. If you love to meet and talk about ideas, you can over-collaborate. If your tendency is to be analytical, you may find you are overly critical of your ideas and may hesitate to implement until things are perfect. If you tend toward implementation and process, you will need to remind yourself that there is a time for creative problem solving and deeper analysis. The important point is that you understand your tendencies and challenge yourself to be counterintuitive.

People Won't Find You!

No matter what your style is as it relates to creating a solution, there is one universal mistake independent consultants can make…believing that people will beat a path to your door if you build a better mousetrap. Time and time again we have seen consultants spend an extraordinary amount of time building a "whiz-bang, newfangled" solution for POTENTIAL clients. Most times this effort is not based on real market intelligence (knowing what people want) but is based on the consultant's belief about what is needed. New consultants often waste the first several weeks, if not months, of their start-up time developing "products," setting up websites, systems, and so forth. And more important, they waste too much of their initial capital because there is no revenue coming in.

You have already spent *years* on your R&D during your career. There is no need to take your precious start-up time to "invent" something, especially if you do not know if anyone wants the invention. If you are inventing cold fusion, go for it. If you are inventing, let's say, a new way to conduct a performance review, don't waste your time and resources. There are plenty of tools out there that can be used and adapted to achieve the desired result. Remember, it is not the hammer and chisel that makes you valuable, it is your skill at using those tools.

I enjoyed the movie *Field of Dreams*. In it, Kevin Costner played Ray Kinsella, a man drawn to build a baseball field in the middle of nowhere. He kept hearing this voice telling him, "If you build it, they will come." He believed it, built it, and the voice was right. However, in the real world of beginning a consulting practice, "if you build it, they will come" is a fantasy! The reality is, "after you sell it, build it," or sell something already built.

Build It and They Will Come – NOT!

Kevin Costner's hearing "build it and they will come" harks back to a very famous Ralph Waldo Emerson quote "If a man can write a better book, preach a better sermon, or make a better mousetrap than his neighbor, though he build his house in the woods, the world will make a beaten path to his door." This is commonly used to justify spending all your time on product development rather than selling. It is usually shortened to "Build a better mousetrap and the world will beat a path to your door." Ironically, the great writer Emerson didn't make his counter-sales point so eloquently. He actually said "If a man has good corn, or wood, or boards, or pigs, to sell ... you will find a broad hard-beaten road to his house." A journalist of the times re-did the quote to the one we know because he thought it had more "punch."

You Must Sell Continuously

Working backwards, this takes us to the first step, sales. The absolute reality is that nothing can happen until an engagement is sold.

We have found that many folks shy away from starting a consulting career because of the need to sell and secure engagements. Professionals who have developed their careers in fields other than sales can take a very negative view of the sales profession. We often hear "I could never cold call" or, "I don't want to come across as a door-to-door salesperson." We also hear things like, "I have no idea where to start," or "Salespeople are born, it is in their DNA." (See the next chapter for more on selling.)

Let me first say that selling is *not* easy. In the best of times, selling can be difficult. It can be darn near impossible if you take a negative attitude toward it and believe sales folks are born, not made. Successful salespeople are no more born into selling than successful human resources professionals, or lawyers, or accountants, or marketing professionals, or...you get the point. People do tend to gravitate toward jobs that reward their natural styles and they enjoy, but sales – like anything – can be learned.

My friend Harvey Mackay (a top author and salesperson) agrees with me that sales is key and you have to commit to learn the skills. When you're selling consulting you're really selling yourself. That's one reason people take temporary rejection so hard. Harvey Mackay says, "All these people out there who haven't had to sell themselves, have to go back and get retrained. What does that mean? That means their lives basically change in two ways: the people they meet and the books they read. They've been out there for 30 years and now they have to switch. They have to sell themselves, go practice the right concepts – and guess what? They will get what they want!"

Some of Harvey's specific advice is:

- Go to Toastmasters. Go to Dale Carnegie for training.

- Read *Dig Your Well Before You're Thirsty*, or any book on networking.

- Learn about selling and learn about expanding your horizons. You think education is expensive, try ignorance.

- Go out and practice the right things you're learning.

(For my complete interview with Harvey Mackay go to http://TAEradio.com/e1059.)

Develop a Sales Process That Works for You

Not only can sales be learned, it is also important to know that sales is more about PROCESS and

STRATEGY than any "gift of gab." Someone following the right process and thinking strategically will actually outperform the "natural salesperson" who is winging it.

The other problem with the perception of sales is the "stereotypical" portrayals of sales in the media. The Blondie cartoons lampooning the door-to-door brush salesman, the Dilbert cartoons insulting the clueless salesperson, and the ever popular "used car salesman" character. Non-sales professionals accept these negative portrayals as the truth and use them as evidence that "sales is not for me."

Again, new consultants must challenge these "truths," and challenge themselves to think differently, and, if necessary, think counterintuitively.

Selling is a process and one that needs to be attended to constantly. Selling is not a light switch that can be turned off and on. You need to implement a regular system to keep prospects in the funnel, previous clients informed, and potential markets aware of what you do. Your process needs to produce regular face-to-face meetings with potential clients. If you don't set up a system you can implement, you are back in the "doom loop" discussed at the beginning of this chapter.

If you'll accept that selling is a process, then you know that there are several steps to any process. Selling is no exception. Depending on how you break it up, a good sales process may have many steps (see the following figure). For your purposes, we recommend no more than five steps. If you can track your target suspects (who you have contacted) plus appointments, proposals and closed engagements that is sufficient for now. (You can see an example of the sales process we use at www.EX3MATTERS.com)

(The following chart is an example of an overly complicated sales process.)

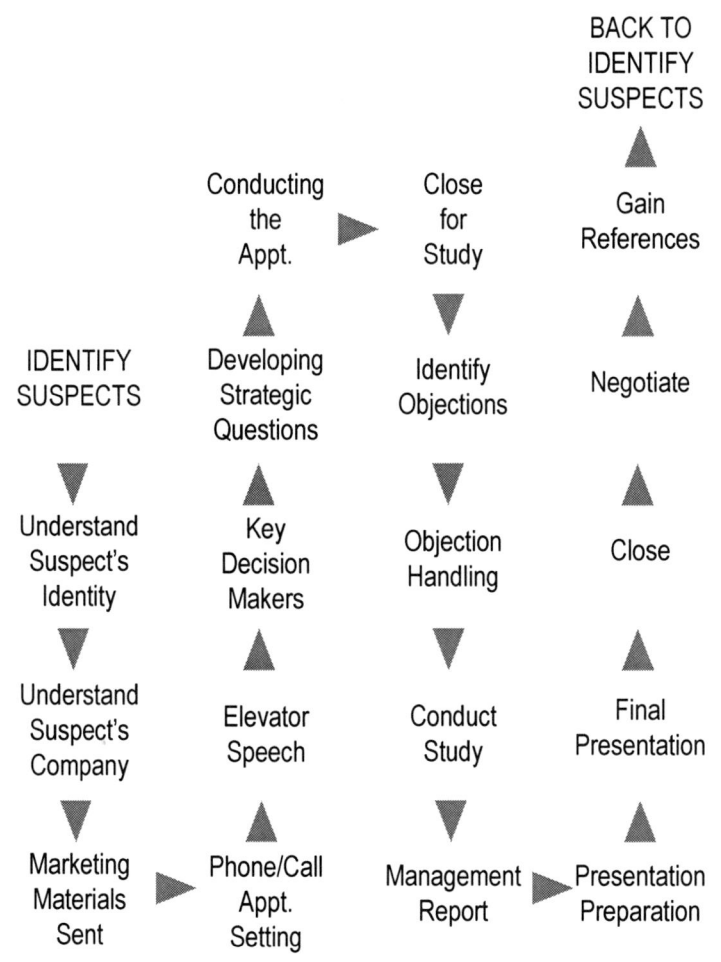

Do not get lost on developing the perfect sales process. The less complicated it is, the better. It is important to have several potential clients in several of the various steps at any one time. This kind of strategy will allow for a steady flow of new work and avoid continuous "feast or famine."

Refine Your Sales System

Once you have a sales process that is comfortable for you, then you can begin to see where you need to spend more of your energy and efforts. For example, if you have several appointments that have not turned into proposals, then you know you need to adjust your sales appointment qualification or your closing techniques. Similarly, if you have several contacts and are not turning them into appointments, then you need to focus on your appointment setting. By monitoring your success at each step, you will have "inputs" to show you where you may need to make some adjustments. World-class performers would call that "game film."

It is important to realize that selling takes energy and it takes more energy for some of us than others. One thing we have learned about folks who do not manage The Cycle effectively is that they go to find new opportunities at the ABSOLUTE worst times possible. As previously discussed, new consultants who have been avoiding sales and have just completed a lengthy engagement are tired. Then they try to sell, which takes a significant amount of energy. Plus, selling, if not made into a process, has a VERY high possibility of failure. Now, take tired people who don't like selling, put them into a situation that requires high energy, add possible rejection and the stress of not having the next assignment lined up, and it is no wonder people fail.

We have seen people give up on their practices after their first successful engagements. On more than one occasion we have seen folks make two or three prospecting calls, not have quick success, and quit right there. They convince themselves it is not going to work, or that they are not cut out for sales, or selling is a negative thing, or any number of justifications that allow them to accept defeat.

The truth of the matter is that they did not work a system. They allowed The Cycle to doom their consulting practices. Instead of breaking the process of sales down into smaller chunks, they tried to tackle it all at once and at the worst possible times. Had they implemented a system that "ate the selling elephant bite by bite," they would have become very successful consultants.

It is rarely the lack of experience, problem solving, or commitment to client solutions that derails a potentially successful consultant. It is the failure to manage The Cycle, and, in particular, the sales process.

Solutions 21 started as a sales consulting practice, so we have a great deal of experience in the selling world. We developed a program, Knowledge-Based Sales™, to position the salesperson as a knowledge source in order to gain an appointment, and ultimately win the client engagement. As I've discussed earlier, *you* are a great knowledge source, so a system like this fits your abilities. Gaining an appointment is the critical step in the process. We have worked with many who say "I am a really good salesperson, if I can just get in front of the decision maker. I can sell better than anyone if I can just sit with them." Well, the fact is, getting in front of the decision maker is the hard part!

If you think you can move the sales process forward once you are in front of someone, then you are halfway home. A good process to gain the appointment is all you need.

We All Have Call Reluctance

When I started Solutions 21 I initially wanted to target sales training and consulting. I had been in sales my entire career and that was the most logical place to start. I had developed a value-added sales approach with my previous employer that had been gaining national attention in the marketplace.

After resigning my position, I was driving home and passed an office for rent. I decided right there to rent a space and not work from a home office. I was convinced that being out in the world was the way to move faster. The quicker I began to sell, the quicker I would know what I was up against.

I spent the first few days pulling my new space together and getting things organized. Then it was "D Day." I had decided that the next day was when I would start calling prospective clients and offering my services. I got to my new office early that morning and was full of excitement. It was before work hours, so calling folks then did not make any sense. I did a few projects until it was time to call and then I sat down with the telephone.

Right when I was about to dial the first number I thought "I wonder if the file cabinets would look better on the other wall?" I walked away from my desk and began to rearrange the file cabinets!! The reality was that what I was REALLY thinking prior to making the calls was "Maybe my prospective clients are going to tell me I should not have quit my day job and they are not interested!"

My call reluctance

I had just quit my job after the best year I had ever had and I was afraid to make phone calls! Instead, for a brief moment I convinced myself to rearrange the file cabinets. Once I snapped out of it, I did go back and make the calls. Some folks hired me and the rest is history.

The point is, even seasoned sales professionals can suffer from call reluctance. We can convince ourselves no one wants our skills or that there is some more important task. We can let our focus stray. There are always reasons to delay acting. But until you have clients, sales are your #1 priority.

From that day on I realized that I needed to implement a *sustainable process* designed to "eat the elephant one bite at a time," even when I felt like rearranging the file cabinets!

Summary

Realize you are delivering results as a consultant and not trading time for money. You have many years of experience (R&D), and your clients are really hiring you to produce a favorable result, not just to spend time. Be careful about "scope creep" and do not give away your years of R&D for nothing.

In order to be successful as a consultant, you must work on all three aspects of The Cycle: selling, creating, and delivery. Most consultants shy away from sales. Don't spend time creating solutions that aren't needed yet. You need a proven sales process that you can implement step-by-step to keep your prospect pipeline full. Then you can create solutions and deliver them, which is what most consultants favor the most!

CHAPTER 4

Selling Your Expertise – How to Leverage Your Knowledge Capital

For new consultants it's important to remember that selling is not a one-time event. It needs to be an ongoing process that is a part of your weekly (if not daily) business plan. Folks who fail to make the sales portion of their practice a regular process are doomed to suffer from "feast or famine." Using a solid process will make the feasts bigger and the famines non-existent. This chapter will discuss the first important steps in the sales process: targeting your market and gaining the sales appointment.

From Good to Great

The first thing you need to do to get started is to focus on "*who* you know." In Chapter 6 we will focus on "*what* you know," but for now we want to look at your contacts.

There is a reason "who you know" is placed ahead of "what you know." There are three reasons why it is critical to create a target list of contacts *before* you fully flesh out your product offerings, the "what you know."

The first reason may be obvious, and we have all

heard it said, "who you know is more important than what you know." I actually only believe this to a certain point. As you start your consultancy, I want to be very clear on this point – who you know will not get you work. Who you know will get you contacts, opportunities, referrals, and introductions. Who you know *is* important. However, at this stage of your career, what you know (and the ability to present it – see Chapter 5) will gain you clients.

As an independent consultant you will be tackling important initiatives for your clients. Your years of experience and knowledge capital are critical to these successes. Your clients are buying "what you know." Who you know is not really all that important once you are hired. Your client will not care about your contacts; they will care about results.

Make no mistake, what you know is critical. Who you know helps. If your contact base is limited you will need to work a little harder than those folks with many contacts. However, with social media and a good plan, it will be entirely possible to make up lost ground on developing your network and contact base.

The second reason we place "who" before the "what" is based upon years of experience. As you will discover in Chapter 6, we consultants often discount our own expertise and knowledge capital. You know more than you think you know.

We have learned that many folks will limit their

thinking about contacts if they have first focused too much attention on the "what." I realize, of course, you would not be reading this book if you have not already spent some time on the "what." However, I would urge you to not limit yourself. There is power in expanding your thinking about *who* can use your skills and *who* might be able to link you to potential clients. Focusing first on the "what" tends to limit our thinking to a far too narrow subset of our contacts.

Finally, in Jim Collins' best-selling book *Good to Great*, he teaches us great companies focus first on the "who" and then the "what." While he is talking specifically about talent acquisition and strategy for companies, the concept applies to you as well. When you put "who" first, your network will enhance your prospecting. People in your network know you and your skills. They will be able to get you to think of additional "whats" you have overlooked.

Targeting Your Market Bull's-Eyes

Looking at your past accomplishments often suggests the type of organizations you can help with your skills. You're probably familiar with the term "target market." Your target market are the prospects that are likely to want what you have to offer.

Many times your skills could potentially help almost any organization. For instance, if you're a team-building expert, any organization from a church to a computer services firm could benefit from better team-work. Or, if you are a sales trainer, even non-profits need to sell to donors.

Friends first

Your initial efforts should target your "bull's-eye." This is the group we call "friends and family." I don't mean friends and family literally, although a few may fall into this group. I mean folks who like you and have a rela-tionship with you already. They may, or may not, have businesses that could use your services. You want to target this group for several reasons. First, this is the safest group to contact. Your friends and family want only the best for you and will allow you to tell your story in a safe environment. They will take your calls. Also, this group may have ideas about where you can go once they know what you are now doing. Using them as referrals will be very valuable as you extend your network of contacts to more prospects.

I describe "friends and family" as those folks who will open their calendars up to you if at all possible. When you ask, "Are you available next week to discuss my new venture?," their response should be, "Let me check; I am sure we can make something work." In other words, it is not a question of IF they will see you, but when. They want to help you. They can be a valu-able sounding board and test market even if they can't hire you themselves.

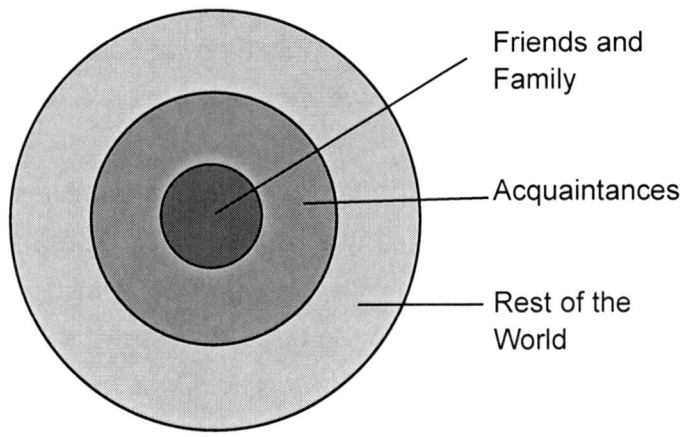

Friends and Family

Acquaintances

Rest of the World

Acquaintances

I call the next group "good acquaintances and contacts." This group knows who you are and may well have a good relationship with you, either from a social situation or from a previous business connection. This group, again, may or may not have businesses that could use your services. What this group does have is knowledge of you. You do not have to prove who you are with them. However, these folks may not immediately open up their calendars and see you unless there is good reason.

This circle of "good acquaintances" may take a bit more work to see. When you ask for time on their schedules, their response might well be, "In regards to what?" One technique to use if they don't want to see you is the informational interviewing technique popularized by Richard Bolles in his book for job seekers,

What Color Is Your Parachute. You ask for their advice; you don't try to sell them. This puts them at ease. They can then give you useful feedback and possible leads to other contacts.

The outer circle of the target is the entire universe of organizations that could use your services. You may or may not have contacts with these groups. It is important that you write down these targeted organizations. It is amazing how powerful this can be. Once you have written down the target you will open up your "reticular activating system." Knowledge about your targeted accounts will be allowed to get through to your conscious self. You will want to add to this list constantly and keep an active list of potential targets.

Your Reticular Activating System

Your reticular activating system (RAS) is in your brain stem and deals with sleep and arousal. It also seems to bring information to your attention that you are interested in. For instance, when you're driving your car "on automatic" your awareness of your surroundings immediately "comes back" when the traffic conditions ahead of you change. Many people have linked the RAS to the power of your subconscious and the idea of positive thinking. For instance, if you decide you want to do consulting for IBM, your subconscious and RAS will bring information about IBM to your awareness.

You will become aware of information you would have previously overlooked. People use goal setting, affirmations, visualization, and similar tools to focus their minds on important information or goals that they want to obtain. This presumably activates their RAS to filter in the information they want.

Partnering With Your Clients

I understand there could be a negative attitude about selling. We have worked with dozens of professional services organizations, from lawyers and accountants to architects, whose education was about their profession, not selling it. As markets have shifted in the past 10–15 years, professionals needed to learn more about business development. I'll show you how you can market successfully in a dignified, comfortable way that fits your personal style.

Most people define marketing as either personal selling or advertising. You may think of selling as pushy, imposing yourself on others, and trying to get prospects to purchase something they don't want.

There's another way to approach sales and marketing. You can serve others in an honest, socially responsible manner. You can improve your marketing without being pushy or using "hard sell" tactics – and you can even enjoy doing it!

If you provide a valuable service, you should be proud of it. You're helping people by letting them know about your services. Why be apologetic, when you can be a passionate evangelist who wants to help others improve their businesses.

Here I'll point out that there are different types of relationships you can have with your clients. Your goal should be to climb to the top of the relationship hierarchy. You can begin to build these relationships at the highest levels even before you do business together.

When you are a VENDOR, you are a commodity. For example, dry cleaners fall into this position when they don't differentiate themselves from their competitors. If you need your suit cleaned, you can go to Dry Cleaner A, B, or C – or X, Y, or Z.

SOLUTION PROVIDERS have a skill that they want to apply. They still aren't focused on what the customer needs.

The CONSULTANT level is the beginning of a long-lasting relationship. You are applying your expertise to understand and solve client problems. (There is more on this and the higher levels shortly.)

TEAM MEMBERS have transcended the barrier of being an outsider. You know as much about your clients' processes as some of their employees and are trusted. If you were a previous employee of the client, you often start at this level.

The term "PARTNER" is often used, but seldom attained. As a partner, you have proven that you have the client's interests at heart. You are privy to high-level

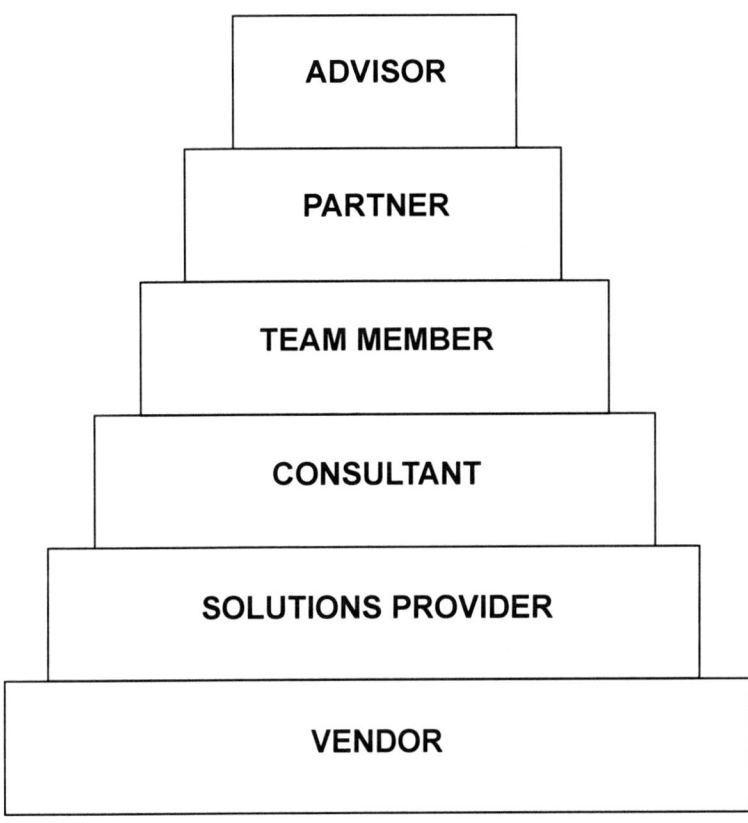

information and do more than you are asked to do. You treat the client's business as if it were your own.

ADVISOR includes all the attributes of the other levels plus the ability to act independently for your client. You take responsibility for their business and often act as a mentor. I am convinced that working at this level is why we have maintained such long relationships with our clients.

While there are many ways to describe relationships between you and your clients, this hierarchy gives you some goals to shoot for. While you can't be at the highest level with every client, you will build the best business – and enjoy yourself the most – when you have clients who trust you at the highest levels.

(Portions of the above section on partnering were adapted, with permission, from *Marketing Your Services: For People Who Hate to Sell* by Rick Crandall.]

Knowledge-Based Sales™

Now that you have focused your attention on your potential target accounts, you will need to make them aware of you! You need to find a way to get your name in front of your targeted prospects. You'll want to do this in such a way that PROVES you are a resource that can be valuable to them. Most marketing and sales programs are designed to set you apart from your competition. Yet competition may not be your problem. Your best potential clients may not even realize they are in need of your services. You need to open their reticular activating system…about you!

Several years ago we developed the Knowledge-Based Sales™ (KBS) system. This system has proven to be very effective in gaining appointments and helping Solutions 21 grow our business. It is based upon some simple truths – today's buyer is a conceptual buyer who never has enough time and can never have enough knowledge or information.

In order to fully appreciate the concept of KBS, we have found that a little history lesson can be useful. There are three major business revolutions that have shaped the way decisions are made. These are the *Industrial, Information,* and *Post-Information* Revolutions.

The development of industry

The Industrial Revolution began in about the 1850s in England. In no time, individuals gained great wealth by leveraging capital and the availability of cheap labor. Many of these folks are well known today as "The Great Industrialists." More than 150 years later, names like Carnegie, Rockefeller, and J.P. Morgan are still familiar to most people. I was familiar with these industrialists from a very early age. I grew up in a small town just outside of Pittsburgh, Pennsylvania, called Homestead. That is where Andrew Carnegie purchased Kloman Steel and developed Carnegie Steel which was sold to J.P. Morgan and ultimately became US Steel, the first billion-dollar corporation in America.

Let's talk about how those industrialists leveraged things into great wealth. The first thing they leveraged was long work days and low wages. Twelve hours days were the norm. Industrialists leveraged the workforce, low wages, and the wave of immigration. At that time a labor dispute was simply squashed and then a whole new wave of immigrants came in and took those jobs. Once labor obtained leverage, conditions improved and you had assembly-line production and better work conditions. All these developments were a product of the Industrial Revolution. That took us up to post WWII and into the mid 1950s. The Industrial Revolution lasted about 100 years.

The Information Revolution

The Information Revolution started about 1957. Most historians agree it started with the launching of Sputnik, the world's first satellite. Sputnik was about the size of a beach ball. It orbited Earth and it "beeped." That's all it did! But, suddenly the "race to space" was on. Because the USSR launched this beeping beach ball, the United States got into the space race. Technology started to advance at a rapid pace, computerization

The History of Bugs

The term "bugs" – meaning problems – has now permeated every aspect of our culture. But it derives from the days when computers took up a full room. Computers like ILIAC and ENIAC ran on vacuum tubes in the early days. They put out a lot of heat and light which attracted moths and other real bugs. At the least these bugs were a bother, and at the most they shorted out tubes. The term has stayed in the language long after computers gave up vacuum tubes.

began to happen, and we saw major industrial businesses evolving. During the Information Revolution, businesses were able to leverage technology to drive their businesses. Originally, only big companies could afford that kind of technology. A computer filled a room. Today, one laptop has more computer power than the old room-sized computers!

The post-information revolution

Today we have the Post-Information Revolution. We talk about things like "digital natives." The Industrial Revolution lasted about 100 years, the Information Revolution maybe 30. The Post-Information Revolution is almost reinventing itself yearly. It's about leveraging technology. Not technology that the *Fortune* 50 leveraged in 1960, but technology everybody has access to that is changing monthly. Think of "apps." The term didn't mean anything to us a year or two ago. Now we look at an iPhone and tens of thousands of different apps are available. Almost instantly it's an entire new technological world. This is critical to us as consultants. Today you can use your creativity, your solutions-orientation, your knowledge, experience and resume in ways that were impossible a few years ago. You are able to provide services now as an independent consultant in a Post-Information Revolution world that only a large organization could have leveraged before.

You Help Clients Cope

Information and new tools are coming too fast for today's decision makers to manage. It is literally impossible for people to know all there is to know about managing their businesses. There simply is not enough time. When you combine the speed of change with the fact that business owners also must balance hectic personal lives, it is easy to see that today's buyer NEVER HAS ENOUGH TIME. To be successful, you need a process that shows respect for the limited time available to decision makers and proves you are a knowledge source that can help them meet their goals. In Kouzes and Posner's seminal book, *The Leadership Challenge*, they explain being a knowledge source this way: "Knowledge is the new economy. Knowledge has replaced land and capital as the new economic resource. Knowledge added is the new value-added whether in goods or services."

As you begin your practice, find a sales process that leverages your position as a knowledge source and not a time waster. We developed and use KBS, which is a marketing concept. This concept is designed to show a conceptual buyer that you will not waste his or her time and that you are a strategic resource. You need to find something similar that works for you. Whatever you choose, make sure it is a system that is easy to implement, allows for constant prospecting (even when you are delivering an engagement), and maximizes the limited time you may have for your sales efforts. Your goal here, in addition to getting clients, is to maximize your sales productivity.

Any sales system you choose to follow must "prove" to your prospective clients you are worth seeing, even *before* you have met them. You will need to maintain a disciplined approach. Your sales and marketing strategy *must* be one that can be implemented regularly *and* while you are delivering client work.

Knowledge-Based Sales Philosophy

Let's talk about the philosophy of Knowledge-Based Sales™ (KBS). Most sales programs that we have seen provide ideas on how to implement consultative sales once in front of the client, but how do you get those initial interviews? How are you going to get people to open the door and see you? We have a full proprietary training course on KBS. I can only provide an overview here that can help you move in the right direction.

You as an information source

You have access to tremendous amounts of information and knowledge. You understand people's businesses and their business challenges. You need to leverage the fact that you have solutions to business problems. You need to show people that you have valuable information before you ever meet them. There are ways to connect with folks before they've met you in person that can convince them that they want to see you. Simple examples of ways to do this are from speeches you do, articles or specific referrals by their peers.

Business partner

The second step is that you can become an active intellectual partner in that person's business. You need to prove to prospects that you are a resource and someone knowledgeable and worth speaking to before you've ever met them. After you've met them, you're going to be able to position yourself as a valuable partner. That ability is going to help you maintain accounts for a very long time if done correctly. You're going to be a resource for those accounts.

Maintaining interest

The next step is to maintain prospects' interest and get them thinking about partnering with you. There are a couple of issues here. You've never met the prospects. How do you get them interested and willing to see you, while not viewing you as a door-to-door salesperson? They must come to view you as the knowledge source. They must recognize your excellence, your valuable experience, and your ability to execute plans. How do you get them to see you prior to their recognition of your real worth? This can be achieved with things like your articles, blogs, and work with similar clients. You can leverage social media and tools to set yourself apart as a knowledge source.

"Juggling"

Finally, how do you maintain their newfound interest while you are working with 5, 10, 15, or 20 clients? You can't be in 20 places at once. So how do you keep folks knowing that they're your top priority while you are with a different client?

I think the critical element of this is acting as a steward of your clients and their businesses. You can provide information to them that they will find useful even if you are with Client A and you can still send information to Client B. That is the critical part of balancing several different clients as once. If you are not selling time for money then giving some focus, every day, to all of your clients is more than acceptable.

It's all about them

Finally, it's all about *them*! KBS emphasizes that no one cares what you know or cares what your resume is or cares what your education is or cares about some intellectual or analytical piece of information that you have. What companies really care about is how all of that can be applied to help them. Don't lay out your credentials, education, and knowledge as a menu expecting them to pick. You need to show that you understand their issues.

Cognitive dissonance

How do we answer the above questions for a more conceptual buyer who is busy and may not want to see you? I'm going to use a term that you may remember from Psychology 101: cognitive dissonance.

Cognitive means the process of knowing in the broad sense. You know something. It fits. It's congruent in your perception, judgment, and memory. You know something. You're cognitively aware. In Psychology 101, this is called cognitive consistency.

Dissonance means lack of consistency. Things don't add up. The pieces don't fit. There is a lack of harmony. It's incongruent.

Cognitive dissonance is an oxymoron. You can't know something and not know something. The human mind, when it's in a state of dissonance, rushes to judgment. Your mind wants to put all of the pieces together. The mind needs to make things cognitively consistent.

Let's explore this scenario. You're at home. The phone rings. Maybe it's the end of your dinner. You pick it up and you say, "Hello, hello, hello." (Dissonance.) What do you do? Most of us hang up. We do this because we know that it's a computer calling us, a telemarketer. In a split second, you have come to that cognitive understanding that this is a telemarketer, and you hang up. You know what the call might be and you move on. Cognitive dissonance is critical because your prospects will try to cognitively place you in the general category of salesperson so they can avoid dealing with you (in a matter of seconds.) You're another sales person. If you do not present yourself appropriately, then your prospect inappropriately comes to a cognitive understanding and thinks that you're a waste of their time. "Why do I want to give you time and take it away from other things I should be getting done?"

We need to use a technique that deals with this mechanism in the human brain. You simply take your marketing approach and position yourself as a knowledge source. You must use this concept to gain people's attention and convince them that you are worthy of getting a little of their time. Then, of course, you show your value to them more explicitly.

Thirty Years of R&D

Over the years I've had the privilege of mentoring several folks who were beginning their consulting practices. I almost always hear the same concern from the aspiring, new consultant. "While I've done many things in my previous career, I don't have any references to give people as a consultant."

One situation in particular has always stuck in my mind. I was talking to a new consultant about using speaking engagements to market her services and she said, "I don't have any experience speaking to these audiences as a consultant."

Not only did she have an advance degree on the subject, she had spoken dozens of times at major international conferences on the same subject while she was employed with her old firm. When she was in the corporate world, she was a sought-after speaker because of her expertise.

In addition to her previous speaking engagements, she was an adjunct professor for a major university and regularly taught a class in her field at the local community college. Her issue was not about content or presentation skills; it was simply one of transferring her previous successes to her new consulting practice. I convinced her it was irrelevant where she had given the speeches and for whom she worked at the time. What was relevant was her expertise and ability to transfer that knowledge to her audience. I advised her to immediately let the "speaking circuit" know she was available and that she had begun her own consulting practice.

Within several months, her speaking calendar was booked solid. The associations that booked her and the audiences that listened did not care who her current employer was…they only cared that she had the requisite knowledge and speaking skills. As you can imagine, these speaking engagements led to many consulting engagements. Even today she continues to do speaking engagements, but the difference is now she is getting paid handsomely to be in front of the room. She gets paid; finds prospects, and the audience members learn valuable information. A true win/win/win situation.

Show Your Expertise

Successful Internet marketers have been using this technique to their advantage ever since the Internet became common place. Blogs, for example, provide valuable information to an audience at no cost. If this information resonates with the audience, then the prospect may well investigate further.

In addition to blogs, many websites gladly give away knowledge and information in order to prove their value. This is done in order to create a *cognitive understanding* that the website/product has value and is worth considering. Even if someone uses the information and does not buy additional products, a positive experience is still achieved. The prospect received valuable information and the provider received a positive interaction with the potential client or reference. A true win/win situation.

As mentioned at the beginning of this section, the above is only an overview of a system we've worked on for years. To summarize from another perspective, the KBS system:

- activates prospects' RAS mechanisms
- leverages your position as a knowledge source
- can be implemented easily, even when you are on client engagements
- leads your prospects to cognitively view you as a resource

Any sales system you choose to follow must "prove" to your prospective clients you are worth seeing, even *before* you have met them. You will need to maintain a disciplined approach. Your sales and marketing strategy *must* be one that can be implemented regularly *and* while you are delivering client work.

Summary

Unless you are so famous that people come to you without any effort on your part, you need to target your markets and apply a sales process. You take prospects out of their state of dissonance when they conclude that you are not a typical salesperson, but a knowledge source. Then they will be willing to engage with you.

Today's buyer is a conceptual and not tactical buyer. Your sales process must focus on the conceptual buyer and not use outdated sales tactics. You are a knowledge source and you need to strategize a process that leverages your knowledge capital.

Websites have been using this technique for years. People cognitively know the website exists to market a product, but when useful information is available for free the buyer is in a state of dissonance. The buyer is in a state of dissonance because the website exists to sell something, not give things away. Once the buyer overcomes the dissonance by cognitively realizing this site is valuable and different, then a transaction usually occurs.

CHAPTER 5

Making Each Appointment Count

As discussed in the last chapter, the most difficult part of the sales process is often getting prospects to schedule an appointment with you. After you have gained the appointment, you need to take some time to develop the strategy you are going to use at your sales meeting.

Buying/Selling Styles

With all of the work that you've done thus far just to get an appointment, the key is to be *completely* aligned. So far, you've found your target markets. You've positioned yourself as a knowledge source. People are thinking of you as having valuable information that could help them achieve their goals. You've focused. All is aligned and you're ready to conduct your appointment. During the appointment you *must* continue to be viewed as a knowledge source and solutions provider.

One of the most important things for in-person selling is to sharpen your skills regarding buying and selling *styles*. People tend to sell the way they personally buy. You will naturally approach a sales situation the way you would like to be approached as a buyer. The only problem with this strategy is that it assumes your buyer has the same style as you.

Also realize that your prospects are most likely in a state of dissonance. They think they understand you want to sell something, but you've presented yourself in a completely different way than usual. This creates a state of cognitive dissonance. They believe you want to sell something, but they also know that you're different.

The human mind wants to rush to a conclusion, wants to get rid of the dissonance; wants to cognitively understand that you are "typical." However, your job is to get that decision-maker to cognitively understand that you are *different.* You're going to help the decision-maker to erase any dissonance by concluding you're worth seeing.

When you are selling your consulting services, it will be critical for you to adapt your style to your buyer's style. For example, I am a bottom-line buyer and can become very impatient with the details. Early in my career I had a very difficult time selling to detail-oriented individuals. I naturally wanted to "cut to the chase" and did not respond well to buyers' detail-oriented questions. My impatience was obvious to the buyers and that was a definite turn off for them.

Early in Solutions 21's existence, we were introduced to DISC profiles. We instantly became a big fan and have since delivered DISC profiles to groups in 15 countries and in eight different languages. (For more information, see ex3matters.com) The profiles have been invaluable for us to understand our natural tendencies for all communications, especially in sales situations. For example, I learned that my impatience is because I am a "D" style (Dominance). In order to become better, I needed to understand the other styles and their buying motivators. I also needed to manage my natural tendencies better in the sales situation. The goal is to ADAPT to the audience in order to become a better communicator. The various styles process information differently and I needed to understand how to ask any questions in a way that produced a productive exchange of information.

The DISC System

There are many well-established and valid personality profiles. My firm recommends and uses DISC, the oldest, most recognized, and most widely used commercial personality profiling program. It was developed more than 75 years ago by Dr. William Moulton Marston.

DISC stands for Dominance, Influence, Steadiness, and Conscientiousness – the key personality traits. I will describe the four primary styles, but most people have a blend of two or even three behavioral styles.

People who score high in *Dominance* are Direct, Drivers, Demanding, Determined, Decisive, and Doers.

They are goal-oriented. They're not shy about telling others what to do. They tend to move fast, talk fast, and think fast. People high in Dominance:

- believe action is critical

- demand results

- may miss emotional cues from others

If the person you are communicating with is high on Dominance:

- Avoid small talk. Get to the point quickly.

- Don't react to their impatience.

- State what you want or need.

- Don't tell them what to do; ask their opinion.

The second DISC type is *Influence.* People who score high in this area are Inspiring, Impressive, Interacting, and Interesting. They are people-oriented. They are socially skilled, persuasive, and friendly. They make people comfortable and are imaginative, optimistic, and can be easily distracted. People high in Influence:

- place a high value on interpersonal interactions

- want to be around others

- thrive on social recognition

- may prioritize socializing over task completion

If the person you are communicating with is high on Influence:

- Be friendly and sincerely interested in them.

- Take time to socialize.

- Use emotional appeals.

- Suggest courses of action.

The third DISC type is *Steadiness.* People who score high in this area are Stable, Supportive, and Structured. They are people-oriented. They are accommodating and peace-seeking. They like stability and supporting others. People high in Steadiness:

- believe task completion is critical

- want to be a part of a team

- are motivated to maintain the status quo

If the person you are communicating with is high on Steadiness:

- Be patient with them.

- Take time to explain things.

- Show an interest in them.

- Give details.

- Don't hard sell an idea.

- Listen more than you talk.

The fourth DISC type is *Conscientiousness.* People who score high in this area are Cautious, Compliant, Calculating, Careful and Contemplative. They tend to be careful thinkers and perfectionists. They are logical, organized and follow rules. People high on Conscientiousness:

- are detail-oriented

- want all the facts and data

- are motivated by being right

- may not handle criticism well

If the person you are communicating with is high on Conscientious:

- Provide details.

- Don't be loud.

- Show that risk is low.

- Don't criticize.

- Don't be blunt.

This is just an overview of the four types. People are often a combination of types and their behaviors are complex. However, you probably recognize yourself in one of these and, with a little practice, you will be able to recognize the styles of the people you interact with in sales and other situations.

Prepare Every Time

Throughout the entire sales process, you need to look for alignment. You need your prospects to understand that you're different. You are a knowledge source. You are worthy of their time. You're not a time-waster. You're someone who can use your skills and abilities to further their business.

During the sales call, you want to ask open-ended, strategic questions that have some depth. As you probably know, an open-ended question is a question that cannot be answered with a "yes" or "no." It requires people to converse – to expand their answers. A closed-ended question can be answered with "yes" or "no." It is a "check the box," "black or white" answer. If you ask, "Are you looking to grow next year?" The answer will probably be a simple "Yes." While that question may have a strategic foundation to it, the question wasn't phrased in a way to elicit useful information. I like to formulate "help me understand" type of questions to get the other person talking.

You need to have your antennae up and read the style of the person you are meeting. You need to be prepared for "what, who, how, and why" type questions. The "help me understand" approach gets me started without using any of those words so that I can better gauge their style. An open-ended question allows the person to continue with the conversation. He or she can offer insights.

Once you get your prospect talking, it is critical for you to capture, as accurately as possible, what your "future client" is saying. You need to take copious notes during the call.

Before you begin asking those open-ended questions, ask, "Do you mind if I take some notes?" I have never, in all of my years, had someone tell me no. The reason? Note-taking honors all of the styles. The high D style realizes that you think what they say is important. The high I style knows that when you're taking notes, you're paying attention to him or her. You're connecting with that individual. The high S style feels safe because you're capturing what they're saying. The high C style realizes that you're being analytical and you're capturing the details of the meeting.

Be exact

Ask your open-ended questions and then wait for the answers. Once they start talking, write down, as nearly as possible, exactly what they say and not your interpretation of what they say. This last point is very important.

Using a client's terminology honors them. Using your interpretation of what they say does not show respect for them. In fact, they might even think you value your own words more than theirs if you interpret what they said differently. Remember that concept. Write down exactly what they say and not your interpretation of what they say. (This also allows you to easily determine what their styles are.)

The second thing is if they say something that's really powerful, impactful, and resonates with you; put it in quotes so that you know it's a quote. Taking notes is one of the most powerful tools you can use in an appointment. Notes are what you're going to rely on when you write your proposal. (Here's another hint: Note taking also forces you to shut up. Most consultants talk too much in an effort to impress prospects. If you're taking notes, you can't interrupt him or her and the information you're receiving just keeps coming!)

Here's one last tip about questions. If you think of a follow-up question as the interview progresses, write it down. Avoid the impulse to interrupt while the person is talking. If you intrude, or if you jump in when they're done or when they "come up for air," you risk losing rapport. You don't want to interrupt or change the topic while they're talking. Just jot down any follow-up questions to ask at an appropriate time.

There are two things I do to prepare before every sales call. First, I write down the open-ended questions I will be asking. Each style responds differently to the phraseology of questions. D's respond to "what" questions, I's to "who" questions (and inclusive pronouns), S's to "how" questions and C's to "why" questions. I write the questions down so I am prepared for any style. Since we all have a tendency to sell the way we buy, and since I am a "D" style, I do not want to fall victim to my natural tendencies and just ask "what" questions. By writing down questions in each style beforehand, I remind myself that my buyer may have a different style than me and I am ready for the other styles.

Example:

D: *What* led you to your current strategy?

I: *Who* helped formulate your current strategy? Tell me about the process.

S: *How* did you formulate your current strategy?

C: *Why* have you chosen your current strategy?

These questions all uncover essentially the same things, but are phrased in such a way that buyers can respond more comfortably depending on their natural buying style.

The Pros Have Always Done It This Way

The most effective people in any profession have always used this sincere sales approach that builds trust with clients. It's funny that many attorneys, accountants, architects, and other professionals in large firms talk like they don't believe in selling. In fact, if the founders of their firms hadn't been able to sell, there wouldn't be any large firms today!

Top professionals ("rainmakers") have always gotten along with clients and brought in business. It doesn't look like they're selling, and often it doesn't feel like they're selling. They are letting people know what they do, impressing people with their demeanor and knowledge, and making themselves accessible. They do this by calling existing customers and keeping the relationships alive, writing articles, giving speeches, following up with contacts, building relationships with referral sources, or meeting new people at trade organizations, churches, or groups. They do it by opening up their target's reticular systems. Then when people have a need, they don't hesitate to call.

Summary

It is natural for people to try to sell the same way they like to be sold. It is important to understand others' buying styles and adapt your questions accordingly. We like the DISC system to understand personality and communication styles (Dominance, Influence, Steadiness, and Conscientiousness). Most people have a blend of two or even three behavioral styles. Despite years of experience selling, I always prepare questions ahead of time that relate to each style.

During your appointments one of the most critical things you can do is take copious notes. This insures you capture all of the information, honors the speaker, connects to every style…and forces you to shut-up and listen! You are there to uncover their needs and not to prove how smart you are.

Remember…"silent" and "listen" have the same letters.

CHAPTER 6

Creating Solutions: Using Your Unconscious Competencies

Once you have convinced a client to hire you to solve one of their business issues, that is the time to begin creating the solution. Notice I said you should begin the creation portion AFTER you have secured the engagement, not before. As discussed earlier, too often people start a consultancy, try to "build a better mouse trap," and then go out to try to sell it. But you should be selling your EXPERIENCE, not a new consulting "product."

Too often a new consultant's time and energy is wasted on building a new product when a tried-and-true product COUPLED with their experience would have done the trick. Several years ago I had a set of golf clubs custom made for myself. Once they were completed, the craftsman reminded me that "it is not the rifle, it's the marksman." The same holds true for your new consulting career. It is not the tool, it is the carpenter.

Another problem with creating products and then looking for people who might need your product is that it makes you a vendor not a service provider. Mack Hanan wrote several editions of a book called *Consultative Selling*. In it he discusses the difference between a vendor selling their inventory of products and a consultative salesperson who becomes a trusted advisor, keeping the client's best interests at heart. Put another way, you don't sell what you want to offer, you sell what the client needs!

Find a Need, THEN Fill It

There are several points you should consider as you build your "tool box" (or product line) as a consultant. Do not build a tool unless you have already sold your consulting to a company that can use it. Control your creative urge to invent. This is not to say you should not invent new things. What I am saying is you should only start the invention process AFTER you have a home for it.

Over the years I have been contacted by many individuals who were starting their own consulting practices. As much as possible, I have always tried to help them get started. My unscientific guess is that 9 out of 10 were spending their precious time and resources trying to create a new solution where there were already good ones available. They were determined that business would beat a path to their door if they only had the perfect tool.

I have always tried to coach folks to go out into the

market and find a home for the new solution first. Sell it, *then* build it. There are two main reasons this strategy works. First is the practical use of your resources. It takes time and money to build a new solution. When you are starting your practice, these are your most precious assets. Manage your time and guard your money. Do not waste either.

Second, inventing is an iterative process. You may think you have a perfect solution, but until you can implement it, you will not see the adjustments it may need. You should have a real client FIRST so you can implement *and* refine the solution. New consultants who don't like the "sell it first" approach often say, "Isn't it unfair/disingenuous to sell a solution that I have not perfected yet?" I ask these folks to think back throughout their careers to a project they have successfully managed. Was it some whiz-bang tool that solved the issue, or was it several tools they used along the way? Most people have solved complex business issues using several tools and making adjustments along the way as needed, versus implementing a perfect tool from the start. There is nothing disingenuous about it. It is simply the way it works. People will be buying your knowledge capital and ability to solve problems, not your new product.

Leading with Products vs. Solutions

Early in Solutions 21's existence, we were introduced

to the DISC Profile. Never having worked with this before, I was intrigued with the tool and found it to be extremely accurate. I was so excited about its possibilities that, unconsciously; I began leading with it in many of our sales calls and proposals.

What I began to realize was that we were branding ourselves as a product provider and not as a solutions provider. People began to refer to us as "DISC trainers." While we were using the tool to solve organizational issues, we were presenting ourselves in such a way as to be viewed as a product provider.

I once heard the expression, "if the only tool in your tool box is a hammer, then everything looks like a nail." If you have a particular tool in mind prior to the sales call, there is an unconscious tendency to lead with that tool. You will subconsciously try to fit the client's issue to your tool rather than solving the client's issue.

There are three primary reasons people spend too much time assembling their tool boxes and inventing new tools. First, there is a fear of getting out there and finding clients. Second, many consultants enjoy the creative process more than selling. Third, many people hear "new tools" and think "retraining." Analogously, author Tom Peters said that many people spend too much time planning and developing and not enough time doing. A traditional approach to doing a job is "ready, aim, fire." Peters said that many businesses use ready, aim, aim, aim, and never act. When you take action, you gain additional information that leads to a more accurate aim than by planning forever. When you're out there "doing," you get more valid feedback to improve your aim. Don't fall victim to this common tendency to over-plan.

Of course you will have tools you've used in your previous work. Take some time to inventory all you have used in the past. It is my STRONG suggestion that you refrain from trying to improve upon them at this point. Just place them in your memory bank for now. Do not buy anything yet. Once you have a paid engagement you will have plenty of opportunity to refine them at that point.

Retooling vs. Retraining

In the early 1980s, the steel industry collapsed and there was tremendous unemployment in the Mon Valley, the area where the mills were located outside of Pittsburgh. Several educational institutions began "re-training" programs to teach displaced steel workers new skills. Many succeeded and began new careers; for example, former "roll hands" learned to be registered nurses. This is "re-training" and it was a truly inspirational thing to witness.

The problem I see with mid-career professionals is their interpretation of "RE-TOOLING." This is not the same as retraining a roll hand to become a nurse.

These are two completely different processes. Mid-career professionals need to understand first and foremost that they are "carpenters." While you may need to learn how to use a cordless air gun, you are still building a house.

Re-tooling Doesn't Require Re-training

Twenty-five years ago my brother Tom and I, in some "brilliant" moment, decided that we wanted to build a log cabin in the mountains. We had never pounded a nail...ever! My dad was a great carpenter so we thought maybe it was somewhere in our genes. We had never done anything like it.

We really learned on the job. Using hammers, electric saws, and all the tools available 25 years ago, we built this house in the mountains.

Here's my point. If we were to build it today, the end result would look the same. What would be completely different would be the tools that we would use. We would still need the same carpentry skills. We would still need to know that "it's 16 inches on center"...all you weekend warriors know what I'm talking about. But we would be using 21st century tools. We wouldn't be using "thumb-buster roof nails." We would be using a nail gun. We wouldn't need to re-train ourselves to build something different. We would just need to understand new tools.

You must know that you are a great carpenter. You have built several very successful "mountain homes" during your previous work experience. It may just be time to re-tool by adding some new tools to the tool box.

Packaging Your Experience

How do you turn your experience into something you can sell? The first step is to realize YOU DON'T KNOW WHAT ALL YOU KNOW.

A concept that you may be familiar with, and that I like very much and use, is conscious versus unconscious competencies. This idea is generally presented as a 2 x 2 matrix:

	Competence	Incompetence
Conscious	**Stage 3** Conscious Competence	**Stage 2** Conscious Incompetence
Unconscious	**Stage 4** Unconscious Competence	**Stage 1** Unconscious Incompetence

Adapted from http://www.businessballs.com/consciouscompetencelearningmodel.htm

Things you're good at and know you're good at are in the first quadrant (stage 3), conscious competencies. Areas where you are aware that you are incompetent reflect conscious incompetence (stage 2) — for example, perhaps you can't play golf well and you're fully aware of your deficiencies. The dangerous area is where you are incompetent but don't know it: unconscious incompetence (stage 1). For instance, you may be a lousy poker player but *think* you are a good player who loses because of bad cards! The area I want you to focus on now is your unconscious competencies: areas where you hadn't realized you have valuable, saleable skills (stage 4).

Analyze Your Experience

You may not think you have any unconscious competencies; after all, surely you know your own skill set. However, many successful consultants don't recognize and value some of the skills that make them successful. For example, many consultants are good not because of having specialized industry knowledge, but because they are confident that they can obtain the information they need, and their projected confidence encourages others to cooperate with them. Or it might be stubborn determination that makes them successful, or their ability to read other people. You may not have focused on why you succeeded in some cases. What I'm looking for here is for you to be clear on factors that help you be successful.

The key to getting your arms around your unconscious competencies is to focus on WHAT YOU HAVE DONE, not where (in what industry) you did it. We often see new consultants falling into the trap of discounting their skills and believing their skills are not transferable from industry to industry.

Analyzing your accomplishments may be more difficult than it sounds. We often don't remember everything we have done in our careers. One strong suggestion we make to aspiring consultants is to use their current resume to help them develop, or at least better understand, all they have to offer as consultants. Take your resume and highlight the accomplishments you achieved in each of your positions. Chances are you have already done this in your resume. Look at each accomplishment in terms of WHAT result you achieved. This is important, but only as the first step.

Now, list each end result you produced. Believe me, when you are done you will feel very proud of your accomplishments and have a much higher sense of confidence moving forward.

My Unconscious Competence

There are several benefits to taking the time to complete the prior exercise. As previously mentioned, you will gain a deeper awareness of not just what you have accomplished, but how you did it, why you chose the path you did, and who benefited from your hard work. Also, if you are like most folks we have helped with this exercise, you will feel much more confident in your past successes.

While all of these points are important, there is actually a much more important benefit in doing this exercise. You will begin to see just how transferable your skills are from company to company and industry to industry. When I first got started, I was convinced my best course of action was to stay in the office equipment world. After all, that was where I started and had my successes. I was a trained and successful salesperson, so my consulting practice was targeted to leverage those key aspects of my resume.

My career had been moving along quite well in sales and I thought my path to retirement was set when Xerox hired me in 1981. After a few years I was recruited to a regional firm in the Northeast and left Xerox. At the new place I became a sales manager, national accounts sales manager, branch manager, and finally the general manager. As a Baby Boomer my career was moving in the direction I had always hoped it would. It looked as if I would work for only two companies in my lifetime.

Something happened though when I became the general manager. Up to that point I had only managed the sales function, and therefore had only really worried about sales. I was convinced that "all roads led to sales" and nothing happened until something was sold. Likewise, I really believed that the sales function was the cornerstone of the entire business.

As general manager my focus needed to change. Now I managed all functions: sales, service, and administration. My world suddenly grew bigger and I began to realize that sales were not the center of the universe. Every area played a key role in our success. In fact, I began to feel bad that I had not seen this before. My strategy changed. Instead of throwing all of our resources into sales, we began to spread our resources out. While we still focused on driving sales, we now invested more in the other areas too. My goal was to break down the age-old boundaries between sales, service, and administration.

We began to focus on different metrics and not just top-line revenue production. Our pretax profits had been traditionally 8%, and the industry average was 7%. At that time, if a business in our industry did 10% pretax profit, they were the "Babe Ruth" of our industry. Our goal was to be the Babe.

With this new focus we formed teams and began to implement an "empowerment program" where decision making was pushed to the most appropriate level. If a service decision needed to be made, it could be made in the field, where the technician really knew what was going on. Prior to this, if a "loaner" copier was needed to replace a unit, it required management approval. Needless to say, this red tape did not reflect a true customer service commitment. It caused delays and had the field technicians questioning whether management trusted their decision making ability..

In addition to spreading our decision making, we addressed the lack of communication between the field sales and service units. We began to track the intelligence provided to the sales department from service. We found that, because in the past sales did not follow-up promptly with service, the amount of information sharing had slowed to a trickle. Service believed their input was not valued and simply stopped giving valuable insights into sales opportunities.

Administration was another issue. We discovered that our sales department would wait until the very last minute to turn in their orders for processing because of the challenges of getting the paperwork processed. It seemed as if sales felt the HARDEST sale was AFTER they secured the order, not getting the order in the first place. Sales resented the fact that their efforts were not celebrated, and administration resented being "put upon" at the last minute. It was a vicious cycle of mistrust and miscommunication. It also showed that neither side understood each others' role and job function.

A "cross travel" initiative was started where everyone spent a day with the functional areas outside of their normal duties. It was important for everyone to understand each other at the human level first. Salespeople processed orders, service techs made sales calls, administration worked in the field with service and sales...in short, everyone worked to learn about "the other guys."

Now, let me rewind a minute. In the office equipment/technology hardware industry, it was ALWAYS about top-line sales. The sales department was the engine that allowed all of the bills to get paid.

My bosses felt that pushing out decision making would dramatically increase expenses because the service technicians would take the "path of least resistance" and offer loaner equipment too quickly without really trying to fix the problem. We were told that cross travel was an expensive waste of time. Also, we were told that sales, service, and administration would NEVER see eye to eye. My bosses didn't like the risk involved in the new program.

Well, I am guessing you can predict "the rest of the story." The new initiatives worked! Customer service scores improved dramatically. The "loaner" expense went down, not up. The "tip leads" from service to sales went through the roof. Paperwork was processed faster, was received by administration "cleaner," and was turned in earlier than ever before.

To make a very long story short, our sales went up "only" 8%, but our bottom-line profit went to 20%! We had doubled the industry benchmark!

From this experience I learned that I enjoyed more than just the sales portion of my career. That is when I decided to start my own firm, Solutions 21. That was in 1994 and I never looked back. Since that time we have grown a great deal. At last count we have worked with hundreds of companies, in 15+ countries. While I never believed I would own my own business, here I am ready to help others do what I've done.

To bring things back to my unconscious competencies, since my background was in sales, Solutions 21 was started as a sales training company. I COMPLETELY discounted everything else on my resume. I believed that if anyone were to hire me, it would be for sales consulting.

The problem was that my industry did not VALUE my accomplishments as much as I would have hoped. My management work on the "empowerment initiative" was downplayed to the point of being ignored. The other problem was, I was calling on previous peers to hire me as a consultant. There was a tremendous reluctance to have me in their businesses, and many times I was viewed as a threat to them in their current jobs. Now, my previous sales results could not be ignored, so several business owners did hire me to teach them my sales strategies – often over the objections of their general managers.

I learned very quickly that it is difficult to "be a prophet in your own land." Before Solutions 21 started I was just like them. Now I was a "consultant." Who was I to tell them how to do something! My first major "a-ha" as a consultant was that the market outside my old industry placed a TREMENDOUS VALUE on the leadership accomplishments and cultural shift that I was able to help shepherd in my previous career. My value as a proven resource to drive cultural change was much higher than my value for sales for most companies.

Now I had two real "products" to sell: sales strategy/ skill development and strategic cultural change. The latter was an example of my own unconscious competency. I'd been aware of it but hadn't thought of it as something to sell.

I was actually shocked to see just how much people were willing to accept us "tapping on the valve" in their firms. Our clients realized great results very quickly based upon our previous years of "R&D." I believe, that is why we still have clients from our early years. Some of our clients have been with us for nearly as long as we have existed. They trust our solutions and continually find "new valves" for us to tap.

Once you are aware of, and comfortable selling, your skill set, you may find that clients are comfortable hiring you in your own industry, including your former employers. You may also find, as I did, that people outside your base appreciate your skills the most. If you look at the previous story, the sales growth was only a small part of the success story. The real success came from the other solutions. I just did not have the insight and confidence to initially see it that way.

Summary

My guess is that you too have similar successes in your background or you wouldn't have thought about being a consultant. You have not progressed in your career by being one dimensional. There are many things you have done to drive results. In fact, I would venture to guess there are so many things you have done to drive results that you have FORGOTTEN some of the things you have accomplished – a variation of the old "I have forgotten more about XYZ than others know" adage. My goal in this chapter was to get these forgotten accomplishments out of your head and into your service offerings. Believe me, you have ideas and solutions that businesses need. Your knowledge capital is very valuable. Leverage it!

CHAPTER 7

Delivering Your Services

You have sold a client on your abilities and created your own solution; now it is time for you to deliver the engagement. At this point it is VERY IMPORTANT to remember the lessons from the last chapter. You don't know all you know! With all of your experience, you are unconsciously competent in many things. So much so that you may begin to believe others know all that you know. Do not sell yourself short. You'll be surprised by what people don't know or aren't perceiving clearly. Your clients are dying for your experience and your competencies. It is up to you to transfer that knowledge to your clients and solve their challenges.

When we are working with senior leadership, too many times we see a lack of solid communication across the board. Leaders too often have a "been there, done that" mentality. As it relates to communication there seems to be a feeling that, "I said it. Don't they get it?" We will often ask a simple question, "Which is more important, what you say, or what is heard and understood?" The answer is obvious. What you say is fairly irrelevant. What is heard and understood is the key.

Being Heard and Understood

Your job as a consultant, and ultimately a change agent, is to be heard and understood. When it comes to the delivery side of your practice, there are several things you need to understand. Rick Crandall, in his book *Marketing Your Services*, talks about "the attention deficit" of human beings when you're marketing to them. "Most people use less than half of their intelligence when reading memos or listening to speeches or reading newsletters. Some people don't read anything, they just ask other people 'what is this all about,'" observes Crandall. "People are distracted, thinking about their jobs, their personal problems, or a myriad of other things. To put it bluntly, most people respond with the intelligence level of a small child to many of your 'important' messages. This means to get your message across effectively, you must be focused. Then you're going to have to repeat it over and over, so that your message has a chance to seep through their distractions."

The same thing is true for your consulting advice and for the people you'll be helping. You simply cannot present a solution and expect 100% compliance and understanding. Even if your clients have that "a-ha" moment, the ideas will fade over time. Your role is to drive past the initial "a-ha" and help the client move to implementation. Not to be cynical, but how many of us have had a moment when we decided to make improvements in our lives? Maybe we decided to lose weight, stop smoking, or exercise more. At the moment of our epiphany, we probably were committed in our minds. We understood we needed to make a change.

The reality is the change required long-term discipline and persistence, not just an "a-ha." Your job is to bring people to the "a-ha" AND then to drive them to the result. This requires discipline and a plan for implementation. In addition, in all of our engagements, we build in what we call "Phase IV" of the implementation cycle. Quite simply, it's follow-up! All of our clients know that after the initial implementation of our solution, there will be systematic and ongoing follow-up to make sure the implementation is reinforced.

Eating the Elephant One Bite at a Time

When Solutions 21 first got started, we were a sales consulting and training company. During our first year we secured a new client who wanted us to train their more experienced sales folks on consultative selling. We were thrilled about the opportunity and customized a really solid program for their organization.

After the initial engagement, the ownership invited us in to talk about several issues they were having organizationally. They thought we might be able to help them in one or two other areas. We met with the owners for a couple of hours and they laid out 15 or 20 challenges they were facing that needed to be fixed. At the conclusion of the meeting, we promised to pull a proposal together and present it for their review.

When we left their offices, we were overjoyed. This was one of the largest opportunities we had seen up to this point. Nearly every area they outlined was within our area of expertise, and we knew we could help.

We pulled together a proposal for their review that had a two-year implementation. Based upon our additional conversation, we made sure to include the "kitchen sink." In other words, we tried to tackle every issue they laid out for consideration. The proposal called for a two-year implementation and was priced in the low six figures per year.

When we reconvened with the owners and went through the proposal, I knew right away we had missed the mark. We overwhelmed them with a solution to every issue they brought up. The implementation looked to be unrealistic to them and they feared a great deal of disruption for the next two years. Needless to say, we did not close that proposal.

After our meeting we conducted a lessons-learned session. It became very apparent that we "tried to feed them the elephant in one bite." Our solution was right on the money, but it was overwhelming.

A short time later we revisited the account and started to dialogue again. This time, in our proposal, we decided to "feed the elephant one bite at a time." With the first proposal, the client simply could not digest everything we suggested. Our new proposal broke our recommendations down into more manageable pieces.

We learned a valuable lesson about "eating the elephant one bit at a time." Due to the changes we made, this client is still with Solutions 21. We have done a project for them, in one way or another, every year for the past 15 years. This client has represented over a million dollars worth of revenue to our company over the long haul.

Our client has grown over 500% in the last 15 years. Their bottom-line profits are twice the industry average, and they are regularly recognized as one of the top performers in their industry. If you were to talk with our client, he would tell you that had we implemented the first proposal, it simply would not have worked in their culture. In fact, we have talked about it many times, and he is convinced Solutions 21 would have been dismissed from the initial engagement in the first six months. We had proposed more change than the organization could absorb.

Our client clearly knows that he has paid us five or six times the amount of the original proposal. He continues to be one of our best references and we can directly link 20 of our other clients to his referrals.

The Advice vs. Implementation Argument

Over the years there has been some controversy about whether it is ethical for a consultant to give advice on what the client needs and then do implementation. It is a conflict of interest if you are motivated to give advice in order to make more work for yourself. In practice, most clients *need* and *want* your help implementing solutions. They trust you and don't want to waste time bringing another consultant up to speed on the implementation. Since our approach is to be a partner to the client, we never have this conflict. If we think outside expertise is needed, we arrange it and help the client coordinate it.

How Change Occurs

In a moment of decision, the best thing you can do is the right thing, the next best is the wrong thing, and the worst thing you can do is nothing.
–Theodore Roosevelt

Creating change for your clients is a major part of what you do as a consultant. I'll overview a few change basics here just as reminders. There are many books on the topic for your further reference.

Planned or forced

Change can be planned ahead of time or forced on your client. An example of the former would be implementing a TQM program or seeking ISO certification. An example of the latter would be when a competitor creates a product that destroys your market or when financial reverses require extensive downsizing. When change is planned, the biggest problem is often getting buy-in from the people the change affects. If things have been going well, it can be hard to convince people of the need for change. As Ken Blanchard, The One Minute Manager, says, this is particularly problematic when top management has tended to institute a "program of the month." When employees see leaders or managers get enthusiastic about new programs repeatedly, they become jaded and tend to keep their heads down until the latest program is ignored for a new one.

A vision must be sold

In order for a change program to succeed, there must be a clear vision of why it is undertaken and the goal that it is designed to achieve. External threats often make for clearer and more compelling reasons to change than planned change. When selling a vision, the communication needs to be clear and simple, even if the complete change process is quite complex. For instance, much "MBA/corporate speak" used in vision statements sounds like "gobblety gook:" "Our goal is to enhance the enterprise structure supporting our external interfaces in order to facilitate the enhanced interchange and flow of information between internal and external nodes...blah, blah." In contrast, you might say "we need to gather input from our customers so we can meet their needs and develop new products for growth." People need to be able to buy in, remember, and repeat your vision.

Many people's first reaction to a call for change is avoidance or resistance. If they are happy with things as they are, they are on station WIIFM. At some level we all want to know "what's in it for me" when we are asked to do something, especially something new. If your goal is to make the company more efficient in order to improve profits, the board of directors might like the goal, but why should the employees care? In fact, employees are going to assume that these changes means potential downsizing or other threats to their situations. It's important to deal with WIIFM. For example, improving efficiency could be coupled with a new bonus program where employees share in pro-ductivity improvements. You could also discuss how expanding the company would create new paths for career advancement.

Champions from the top and bottom

A change program that a consultant researches and develops will sit on a shelf if it doesn't have internal champions. For any serious change to take place, someone in the company must be emotionally involved – they must really care about its success. Normally this requires someone at the top, and this champion must repeat the message over and over, long past the time when those who welcome the change have started implementing it. Interestingly, a change champion can come from anywhere on the organizational chart. Those on the front lines can initiate programs and even push them without top support in some instances. Of course the best cases are to have champions at all levels and in all departments. The visions that achieve this are often more "unselfish." That is, they are not just to improve profits but are improvements that benefit everyone. For instance, seriously improving customer service makes customers happier, the jobs of the front line who work with them more pleasant, and corporate profits higher. (For more on this, see the Bain/Reichheld programs that show improving customer retention by 5% can improve profits up to 100%.)

The road map

In order to achieve a vision, you have to have a road map of sorts. There are many computer programs that create charts that lay out the steps you think you need to create change. Many folks don't like the details of planning. When working with consultants, they think planning sessions are a waste of time. They want you to be implementing because they "see" the goal so clearly and "know" how to get there. Even when you have a detailed plan, you should expect the plan to change. Some people have "analysis paralysis" that delays their taking action. They're sure that if they just study things a bit longer, they will implement better.

As I've indicated throughout this book, my bias is toward action. When you take action, you learn more than from thinking things through for the fifth time. Most implementations require more time to get people on board than they do to implement "physically." The models that think of organizations as machines where you can tinker with the gears are not correct. Organizations are more like living organisms. There are connections, "hormones," and feedback loops that are not visible on an organizational chart. They're messy, not mechanical or clean. So develop a plan of action, but test it slowly, take time to get buy-in, and expect to make iterative changes as you go along.

Dealing with resistance

It's generally easier to keep doing things the way you're used to than to change. When change is someone else's idea, people will resist both passively and actively. They may simply be waiting to see how serious you are about the change. They may be waiting to be consulted personally for their input, or they may quit rather than deal with the change. To oversimplify, generally about a third of people like change, a third hate it, and a third are ambivalent. When you have the change enthusiasts on your side and the neutral people not objecting, you may think your problems are over. But resistance can remain for an extended time.

Change can be analagous to a death in the family. People may need time to go through the stages of grieving for the good-old days. If handled with respect, most resistors will become supporters for a well implemented program. As a consultant you need to be constantly aware of the need to balance two critical elements – leadership's impatience and demand for results, and the organization's natural push-back.

Creating Personal Change

The change techniques you use for clients also work for personal change if you apply them. However, most of us are better at helping clients change than we are at helping ourselves! Personal change can involve anything from exercise, to relationships, to starting a consulting business. Planning is fine but don't overdo it. As already mentioned, Tom Peters said, most people do "ready, aim, aim, aim" and never act. You're better off with "ready, fire, aim." By taking action you gain more information to improve both your planning and action. If you're considering a change, taking some preliminary action gives you both useful feedback and momentum for further action.

Your Influence

One key area for new consultants to understand is how to develop your influence. In our work with leaders we try to point out the two key kinds of "power" available to them. First is "position power." Simply because they are the boss leaders have position power. They can ORDER people to do something because they have the title. The next type of power, and the one that is MUCH more impactful, is "influence power." In this case, people do things because they WANT to, not because they are ordered to or have to.

As a consultant, and an outside resource, it will be VERY RARE that you will have clear position power in the client's organization. By definition, you are an outsider and do not have direct reports you can order around. You WILL have some degree of position power. Folks will know you are there to tackle an issue and that someone near the top hired you. You have indirect position power through the "bosses." However, let's focus on the folks who hire you, not the folks who report to them.

New consultants sometimes have a hard time realizing they cannot order anyone to do anything. Many of us were bosses in a previous life, and we did get people to do things "because we said so," even if we hate to admit it. In your new life as a consultant, you must work on your *influence* power. This will require you to continually develop your communication skills. Also, you will want to create a network of peers so you can strategize solutions with a like-minded group. If you are a person who likes to talk through ideas, you will need to realize who you can talk to…and who you should NEVER include in your "brainstorming."

Remaining Objective and Driving Results

One of the biggest and most frequent mistakes new consultants make is to start thinking of themselves as "an employee" rather than a "trusted advisor." Since many new consultants are "solopreneurs," and by definition work alone much of the time, there is a tendency to reach out to your client's employees as a way to create community. The *Urban Dictionary* defines solopreneur as "entrepreneurs who work solo running their businesses single handedly." They might hire contractors, yet they have full responsibility their businesses.

It is CRITICAL for you to maintain your independence and objectivity. You must avoid The "Stockholm Syndrome" at all costs. Using the Stockholm syndrome as an analogy may be harsh (see sidebar), but the point is valid. You are an independent consultant and your objectivity is critical. You can't identify too closely with client's issues. If you begin to view some of the dysfunction that you have been hired to correct as OK, then you will not be successful.

The Stockholm Syndrome is when people held hostage begin to have positive feelings for their captors. They begin to identify closely with them. Sometimes they even seek contact with them after they are freed. Patty Hearst who was kidnapped and then joined the gang that kidnapped her would be an extreme example.

Another big mistake new consultants make is assuming their clients' dysfunctions. Early in Solutions 21's existence, we would find ourselves sitting around the conference table talking about solutions for our clients. The conversations would often become not solution oriented, but a commiseration about our client's issues. I remember one time in particular when we were working with a family business that had four equal owners. The four siblings had issues with each other, and each tried to get us on their side in the various disputes. Instead of us confronting the issue and facilitating a discussion with the owners, I must admit that we allowed ourselves to be pulled into unproductive conversations.

When we would get together as a team, we tended to waste far too much time and energy discussing the dysfunctional issues our client faced rather than remaining solution-oriented. This was a waste of time and energy. Everyone has issues. Also, and even more important, if our clients did not have challenges, we would not have clients! We need to confront the practical issues head on and find a solution. (The good news is we learned quickly and this client is STILL a client and their business has grown an incredible 1200%)

I dislike speaking in absolutes, but there are some instances where it is appropriate. Always, always, always focus on solutions and results. Do not waste time and energy commiserating. As discussed in Chapter 2, World Class Performers practice energy management. You will find that your energy is one of your biggest assets, and it needs to be focused on results.

Finally, use an outside network of peers rather than your client to help with your brainstorming and getting fresh ideas. As German Chancellor Otto von Bismarck is supposed to have said, it's better if people don't see the process of how sausages or laws are made! Clients expect solutions and results. They want the sausage. They do not need to know (or see) how the sausage is made.

Using Tools

If you need to purchase tools, look for ones that can be used in many ways and are not one dimensional. Solutions 21 uses a wide range of tools and we often use the same tool for very different engagements. For example, earlier I discussed the DISC tool. This is a wonderful tool that we use in engagements ranging from sales consulting to strategic plan development.

The tool is very versatile and helps people understand themselves and others better. There are literally hundreds of applications. We have used this tool in working with clients for over 15 years and have added to our depth of understanding along the way.

As you build your toolbox, avoid any "one size fits all" tools. While I have mentioned DISC often, that is not the only tool we use. We have many profiles and assessments that we can use on almost any engagement. Whether we are doing a strategic plan, process redesign, or a leadership program, we have a tool that works to drive the result. The information these tools provide and the "a-ha" moments you can achieve will help you drive your solution in a disciplined and meaningful way.

One of your most precious assets is your capital, so only buy tools when you need them. When I first got started, I wish someone had given me this advice. I wanted to have EVERYTHING...NOW! I bought too many things at once, thinking it would give me a competitive advantage. All it gave me was a large credit card bill and a headache!

By the time I was ready to use some of the tools I had purchased, I had discovered better solutions. Also, for the tools I did end up using, if too much time had passed, I needed to re-familiarize myself with their uses. I had forgotten how to use them proficiently. Think of buying a language immersion program. You may be able to learn and speak the language, but if you do not use it regularly much of your skill will be lost. You need to use it quickly and repeatedly in order to maintain the skill.

Listen to Michelle

Six months after starting my consulting practice, I hired my first employee, Michelle Cerqua. Michelle is still with the company to this day and possesses an extraordinary amount of institutional knowledge about our firm. Truth be told, we would have even more documented procedures if I had been smart enough to listen to her in the beginning.

One of our tools, the Innovation Profile, shows your natural style within an innovation process. The five styles are Creator, Advancer, Refiner, Executor, and Flexer. Each style approaches the innovation challenge differently. I learned that I am a Creator. My strength is not in documentation or process development.

When Michelle joined Solutions 21, one of her first suggestions was to document all of the programs and processes we were putting together for our clients for our own internal use. I thought this was a great idea but...

The issue lies with that "but." "But we didn't have time, but there were other things to do, but we would never use that again, but we were just experimenting." But, but, but, but...

Document your work

The reality is, Michelle was right. Over the years we have spent far too much time reinventing the wheel instead of having a clear process to repeat. We should have leveraged the winning solutions we already created better and not reinvented so much.

My advice to you is, listen to Michelle. Once you have created a solution make sure you have a mechanism to document your process and maintain the work product. As much as possible avoid re-inventing the wheel. If you're like me, a Creator, this is completely counterintuitive. By nature we enjoy the creation. However, of the things that I would do over if I could, this would be #1 on the list.

I hate to think of the enormous amount of time we have wasted reinventing the wheel. As an independent consultant, your time is a precious commodity. Do not reinvent the wheel. Listen to Michelle!

If you are purchasing tools, look for opportunities to interface with REAL PEOPLE who have used the tools effectively in the past. I say *real* people because there are many products on the market that have Internet support, and that is fine as far as it goes. There will be times when you will be looking at nuanced issues and having someone (or several someones) to guide you who have used the tools and experienced similar situations is hugely valuable.

Change Takes Patience

As discussed in previous chapters, building rapport with prospects, convincing them that you are a valuable knowledge source, and getting hired takes patience. You need to build relationships with the people in companies who can use your help, and that takes time. Once you're working within client organizations, the need for patience continues. Just because they hired you doesn't mean that they are ready to let you loose to do the things you think should be done.

You will usually be hired to undertake a specific project or solve a particular problem. But the full scope and details of most engagements are seldom completely detailed. As discussed, rather than getting caught up in analysis, you need to define the small steps you can take now that will create progress on the job and give you more information for more refined action. Remember along the way that it is very important to build rapport with everyone you come into contact with. You may know a lot of what needs to be done, but you can't just push the solution through. Other people will have useful information now and for the future. Make friends.

Consulting isn't about waving a magic wand and creating change just the way you want it. It's about careful steps that build to the solution. Let's take the extreme case and say you know exactly what needs to be done in complete detail. The organization will still not be ready to accept everything at once. Only so much change can be implemented at once and you need to build trust for your approach to be accepted. As mentioned earlier, people have reasons for resisting change and their lack of comfort with you is another reason. Be patient. Help them learn to trust you. Even if you "know it all" at the beginning, you'll learn a few things along the way as implementation takes place.

Still a Bite at a Time

The more common case than your knowing everything at the beginning is when the problem and solution are not completely defined. Just as you shouldn't invent tools before you sell them, you shouldn't worry that you don't know everything possible about the issues before you start work. Consultants don't know everything, but they know how to get answers. As you may have noticed, one of our favorite metaphors is "eating an elephant." When you have a big job, like eating an elephant, it can be overwhelming. Be patient. Start with small "bites" that you know will fit the task. As you move forward, new steps will become apparent. As the Chinese saying goes, a journey of 1,000 miles begins with the first step. Each step takes you closer to your goal and gives you a new viewpoint. Meanwhile, you are also building trust in those around you who will contribute to your solutions.

Summary

If you're involved in a change effort – formal or informal, business or personal – the best thing you can do is make your decisions based on the information you have and take action. Your action will give you feedback that you can use to adjust your course. That's the way it happens in a complex world even when you're guided by a focused vision.

Recognize that you have to "sell" changes to employees, customers, and stakeholders. Change creates some losses for people. You need to show the gains. Develop a clear positioning statement. Will your audience respond best to changes driven by speed, customer service, values, or something else? For big, negative changes like downsizing, I recommend making the changes all at once. For organizational culture changes, it's best to incrementally introduce small steps that revolve around one main idea. In either case, start taking action quickly to get momentum on your side. Then use the results to guide your next step.

CHAPTER 8

Is Consulting for You?

If you were to boil down what Solutions 21 does, it would be to:

- help our clients plan (create a vision and tactics to achieve it),
- align (their people and process), and finally,
- execute the plan (get it done!).

We may not work with a client on each step. For example, a client may already have a plan and we might come in to work with them on aligning their processes. The bottom line, though, is that our clients are aligning their processes in order to drive a plan they have developed (formally or informally). What we do is help our clients execute and drive results. We help our clients create better futures.

Seeing the Future

Whenever you are working on a "future state," it is critical to understand what that state will look like. From a leadership point of view, it is critical to create the vision. We have all heard it is a leader's job to create and communicate a compelling vision of what the future holds.

Everyone knows how important it is to have a compelling vision and yet so many businesses do not have one. I am not talking about the "plaque on the wall" vision. I am not talking about the vision statement that was framed and no one even knows about it or, worse yet, people do know about it and make fun of it. I am talking about a REAL picture of what can be…what a better future actually looks like.

It is our job to help leaders "see the future." We need to get them to FEEL what it will be like when they succeed – no small feat for them. This is no small feat for anyone. I deeply believe that a failure to see what CAN BE is a major reason many very experienced and talented folks do not pursue a career in consulting. They lack a vision of what a future as a consultant can be Just as business leaders need help with crafting a vision, you may also need help to "see" what can be. More important, you may need to EXPERIENCE what it will FEEL like when you succeed.

We often use an exercise to get individuals and groups to "see the future." It is the Rip Van Winkle exercise. We have folks pretend they have been asleep for three years. They wake up one day and go to the office. For the past three years everything has gone perfectly. They have achieved all of their goals. All of the constraints were removed and all of the hurdles have been overcome. We ask them to describe what they see.

(For worksheets on this exercise go to ex3matters. com.)

After this discussion we then ask them how it FEELS in this office. How are people acting? What is the atmosphere like? Describe the energy. We have them write down adjectives to describe what they are feeling and seeing. We always hear words like exciting, energizing, meaningful, successful, and happy. Once people begin to FEEL what a better future can hold, then it is easier for them to "see" the future.

What Do You Want?

How about you? Have you taken the time to "see your future"? Have you stopped to think about how you would feel WHEN you are a successful consultant? Have you put positive images in your mind, or have you only put in questions and road blocks?

I am not a psychologist. Far from it. In many ways I am too results-oriented. Too many times I am overly focused on the task at hand. Seldom do I naturally take time to enjoy the moment. I say "naturally" because I have figured out that world-class performers learn when to act counterintuitively. Intuitively I may want to do one thing, but now I know that it may be the wrong thing. What feels right may well be wrong. While I may not yet be world-class, I continue to work towards it.

I say all of this because not so long ago I would have laughed if someone had me do the Rip Van Winkle exercise. I would have dismissed it as a waste of time. Not any more. I have seen clients go from bankruptcy to extraordinary profits in a short period of time. We have seen firms grow 1700%, businesses spun off, firms go public, new products developed, cultures changed for the better, and many other unbelievable achievements...all because leaders and their teams took the time to see a better future and to feel what that future would look like.

It is the same for you. You need to take some time to see what the future can look like for you.

Positive Thinking

In order to envision your future, you may need to challenge some long-held beliefs. In our work with leaders we often need to challenge them and their teams to rethink things they hold to be true...that are not!

Human beings act based on what they believe to be true, not necessarily because of what IS true. Many beliefs we hold about ourselves are often "self talk," and we have convinced ourselves it is a "truth." It may be "our truth," but it is not THE truth. For whatever reason, we may have convinced ourselves of something that is in no way, shape, or form based in reality.

Have you ever thought "I could never...(fill in the blank)." If you have, then you have created a self truth and a belief that may not at all be true. For example, people have often told me as they thought about being an independent consultant, they said to themselves, "I could never sell something." That self talk created a belief that they now hold to be true. The fact of the matter is, they have no idea if they could sell. They've programmed their brains that they cannot sell, therefore it must be true.

If you are considering becoming a consultant, have you thought while reading this book, "I could never find six clients who need what I can do"? If so, and you do not challenge that belief, then it will become a truth for you. If that happens then guess what, you WILL NOT find six clients. Now, let me challenge that thought. In all of my years I have never met a six-figure earner

Failure = Practice

Many people think that if things don't work out exactly as they PLANNED, they have failed. As it turns out, most successful entrepreneurs have failed several times before they succeeded. Early "failures" are simply learning experiences if you keep going and try other approaches. As we get older, we are often more hesitant to try something new that has a learning curve. In other words, if we're not good at something immediately, we tend to quit. We've "paid enough dues" already. Selling consulting services gives you lots of chances to "fail" as you approach different people who don't say yes. But, in fact, it's all practice until you find the right approaches and the right prospects. Perhaps that's why it's called a consulting "practice!"

who did not have AT LEAST SIX important projects in process at any given time! In a corporate setting most people regularly maintain at least six major internal clients.

The reason it is so important for you (and the business leaders you work with) to challenge your long-held beliefs is because the subconscious mind DOES NOT ARGUE BACK. When you tell yourself something negative about yourself, your subconscious accepts it as fact. If you say to yourself, "I could never sell," your inner voice does not say "Don't be silly, of course you can. How about that major project you sold to the international team when they thought they wanted to the exact opposite approach? " It does not work that way.

What you say to yourself is accepted in your mind as FACT, even if it's far from one. As you have considered the career choice of independent consulting, have you thought, "I could never work on my own," "I could never sell," "I don't have enough transferable skills," "I am not a good communicator," "I am not detailed enough," or any other negative thoughts? If so, you may have programmed your mind – incorrectly, I might add – so that you actually cannot do those things. The truth is, you just might be great at those exact things if you tried.

We seldom send our brains words of encouragement. More often than not we send ourselves negative messages. Unless you are intentional about what messages you send to yourself, chances are you have unintentionally placed limiting roadblocks in your way.

> **encourage** [en-kur-ij] *verb*: to put courage into
>
> The word "encourage" implies that when you encourage yourself, you are giving yourself courage. As a bonus, you're also making yourself more cheerful and able to face challenges.

You and Planning

Another challenge that holds back prospective entrepreneurs and would-be consultants is their previous experience with business/strategic planning processes. In many instances 20+ year professionals have been involved at some point in a planning process.

The typical scenario will have a group of leaders and managers getting together to map out their future. One of the tools used in a strategic planning process is a SWOT analysis (strengths, weaknesses, opportunities, and threats.) Oftentimes when someone is starting out and thinking about developing their plan, they refer back to tools like a SWOT analysis that they had used in the past. The challenge is this process works far better in a group setting, especially when a professional facilitator is involved.

A SWOT analysis, if not conducted properly, can

easily leave a group feeling discouraged. This is espe-cially true for individuals who are trying to use this tool by themselves. There is a tendency for individuals to quickly address the strengths and opportunities and make a fairly superficial list of their key differentiators.

Once the strengths and opportunities have been glossed over, the focus then turns to weaknesses and threats. Left unmanaged, too much energy is spent on weaknesses and threats. This can really be discour-aging if it is not properly balanced by strengths and opportunities.

Appreciative Inquiry

Solutions 21 facilitates dozens of strategic plans every year. Our work has ranged from creating new prod-ucts for brand name consumer goods to start-up orga-nizations. We do, in fact, use SWOT analysis when appropriate.

We also use another technique that I think would be much better for folks who are considering becoming an independent consultant. The technique is called "Appreciative Inquiry" and it was developed by Dr. David Cooperrider from Case Western University (http://weatherhead.case.edu/professional-development/certificates/appreciative-inquiry).

Appreciative Inquiry brings out what is possible in an organization by thinking positively. The idea is to craft positively phrased questions that allow us to focus on possibilities. The human mind will be more creative, innovative, and productive when focused on positive outcomes versus taking negative and critical positions. This is also part of the basis of brainstorming sessions.

Earlier in this chapter I shared part of that technique when discussing the Rip Van Winkle exercise. As you consider a career as an independent consultant, how about asking yourself different questions? How about asking yourself, "If all constraints were removed, what would it look like for me in three to five years if I were a successful consultant?" or, "What skills have I developed throughout my career that are valuable in the marketplace?" or "How would it feel in three years when I have a successful consulting practice?" You have to see it and feel it. You have to ask yourself the right questions to get to the best answers. You may also need to challenge long-held…and untrue…beliefs about yourself.

Unlimited Potential

In 1994 I would have never dreamed of being asked to do some of the things we have done. I would not have allowed myself to think such encouraging thoughts. Hiking a remote part of the Great Wall of China with clients was what other people did – not me. I was a copier salesperson.

Well, I was wrong. I held self-limiting beliefs that simply were not true. I am fortunate that circumstances and experience have proved me wrong. I have also been fortunate to have taken this leap long ago.

Believe me, if I can do it, so can you. Success as an independent consultant is *not for someone else*. It is for you, if you commit to it. You have to commit 100%. No looking back. Do not dip your toe in the water. Once I decided to start Solutions 21, I came across a quotation by William Hutchinson Murray. It has hung on my home office wall ever since.

COMMITMENT
Until one is committed, there is hesitancy,
the chance to draw back, always ineffectiveness.
Concerning all acts of initiative (and creation),
there is one elementary truth, the ignorance of which
kills countless ideas and splendid plans:
that the moment one definitely commits oneself,
the providence moves too.
A whole stream of events issues from the decision,
raising in one's favor all manner of
unforeseen incidents, meetings and
material assistance,
which no man could have dreamt
would have come his way.

Summary

If you have valuable experience, most of the things that will limit your ability to build a consulting career will come from within you. All of the indicators in the market point to a huge demand for experienced professionals. Businesses just want to acquire the talent differently. If this feels right, do it. Don't wait. Commitment is a powerful thing.

If I can help, please go to ex3matters.com. See the "contact" page or connect with me in the social community. Looking forward to hearing from you.

Buddy Hobart

JOHN W. "BUDDY" HOBART
President and Founder, Solutions 21

Buddy Hobart founded Solutions 21 in 1994 with an initial focus on sales consulting and training. Today, the Pittsburgh-based firm is a global enterprise that provides services in four primary practice areas: Client Development, Enterprise Learning/Human Capital Management, Strategic Planning, and Process Improvement. Hobart has taken his extensive experience as a consultant and launched Ex3 Matters, a business designed to help professionals launch their own independent consulting practice.

Hobart has led Solutions 21 in providing leadership and management solutions to companies around the world, ranging from start-ups to Fortune 500 enterprises. Hobart is the creator of the Knowledge-Based Sales™ consulta-tive sales approach, which has dramatically transformed sales revenues for companies of all sizes around the world. Furthermore, Hobart's unique application of the World-Class Performers model has armed leaders with the tangible tools that allow them to implement and sustain successful change in their organizations.

Hobart's first book was *Hire Education*, designed to teach college students how to successfully present and market themselves as they enter the workforce. *Celebrate Selling the Consultative-Relationship Way*, which he co-authored, provides a compilation of works for the sales professional. And *Gen Y Now: How Generation Y Changes Your Workplace and Why It Requires a New Leadership Style* discusses how leaders can adapt to a rapidly changing workforce to obtain a strategic advantage by properly leveraging Generation Y talent.

Hobart has appeared on television, radio, and in print, sharing his expertise with *The Wall Street Journal, USA Today, Chief Learning Officer*, and other business publications. He is a frequent and returning speaker at industry events and leadership forums around the world such as the Young Presidents' Organization. He also hosts a radio show, *The Consultant's Corner*, which explores the factors and trends that have an impact in today's business environment.

Index

CPSIA information can be obtained at www.ICGtesting.com
Printed in the USA
BVOW081419160712

295326BV00003B/1/P